TALKING ABOUT ABOLITION

TALKING
ABOUT
ABOLITION
A POLICE-FREE
WORLD IS
POSSIBLE

SONALI
KOLHATKAR

FOREWORD BY
ROBIN D. G. KELLEY

SEVEN STORIES PRESS
NEW YORK · OAKLAND · LONDON

Seven Stories Press
140 Watts Street
New York, NY 10013
www.sevenstories.com

College professors and high school and middle school teachers
may order free examination copies of Seven Stories Press titles.
Visit https://www.sevenstories.com/pg/resources-academics
or email academic@sevenstories.com.

Library of Congress Cataloging-in-Publication Data is on file.

ISBN: 978-1-64421-435-0 (paperback)
ISBN: 978-1-64421-436-7 (ebook)

Printed in the USA.

9 8 7 6 5 4 3 2 1

"Abolition is a mandate to create new social, economic, and political conditions that will render carceral punishment obsolete. It is a mandate for revolution."

—ANGELA Y. DAVIS

CONTENTS

GENUINE ABOLITION
REQUIRES A REVOLUTION

BY ROBIN D. G. KELLEY

Sonali Kolhatkar chose the perfect title for this book. *Talking About Abolition* echoes Tracy Chapman's iconic song "Talkin' Bout a Revolution." Chapman predicts "Poor people gonna rise up / And take what's theirs." It is perhaps the oldest and most pervasive prediction in history besides the ancient prophecy of end times or planetary destruction. We are living through an era when "abolition" and "revolution" are used almost interchangeably. Both are often presented as processes that will resolve humanity's most pressing contradictions; both are means toward liberation. Of course, they are not the same thing, and the meanings of abolition and revolution are hardly settled. However, I would argue that today's abolitionists, epitomized by the thinkers and activists contained in this book, are also today's revolutionaries.

Genuine abolition requires a revolution. It entails ending the array of carceral and gendered racial capitalist institutions that dominate our lives and render much of humanity insecure and vulnerable to premature death. Abolition demands a reordering of things by redirecting resources from prisons, police, and the military toward education, universal healthcare, housing, living-wage jobs, and green energy. It demands a system of transformative justice free of cages, torture, banishment, and death:

a system grounded in the principles of accountability, care, and repair. Abolition must be feminist, anti-racist, anti-nationalist, and anti-ableist. It must be committed to eradicating all forms of oppression, exploitation, and violence and to freeing the body from the constraints of inherited and imposed normativities. Abolition must be committed to eliminating borders and protecting the Earth.

Sonali is a skilled and sensitive interlocutor, possessed of political clarity and a wellspring of historical knowledge. She draws from her conversations with these twelve extraordinary revolutionaries a rich, nuanced, and thoroughly convincing argument for abolition: what it means, why it is necessary, and how it is possible to achieve. She ends by reflecting on her friend Dortell Williams, an incarcerated Black man who, in many ways, is the inspiration for this book. I think it is safe to say that, for everyone featured in *Talking About Abolition*, the people trapped inside and those whose lives have been stolen by the system have always been the primary force driving their work in the abolitionist movement. Just as the first abolitionists arose from the ranks of the enslaved themselves, imprisoned intellectuals and victims of relentless state violence were modern abolition's original visionaries. They have been thinking, dreaming, and talking about abolishing the carceral system since it came into being. Some built a case for abolition from the Koran or the Bible, citing the promise of Jubilee as told in Isaiah 61:1-2:

> The spirit of the Lord God is upon me
> Because the Lord has anointed me;
> He has sent me to bring good news to the humble,
> To bind up the brokenhearted,
> To proclaim liberty to the captives and release to those in prison;
> To proclaim a year of the Lord's favor and a day of vengeance of
> our God.

During the 1960s and '70s, a generation of imprisoned intellectuals made sense of their daily, dehumanizing encounters with the carceral state through radical critiques grounded in Third World revolution, Marxism-Leninism, anarchism, Black nationalism, and their participation in Black rebellion. They called themselves prisoners of war, regarded police as an occupying force in Black and Brown communities, and understood the prison as a tool of counterinsurgency. Resisting state violence, more than outright abolition, was their main focus. They formed or joined organizations such as the Revolutionary Action Movement, the Black Panther Party for Self-Defense, the Community Alert Patrol, the Black Liberation Army, the Brown Berets, the National Committee to Combat Fascism, and the Third World Women's Alliance. George Jackson, Angela Davis, Martin Sostre, Mumia Abu-Jamal, and many others developed critiques of captivity, opening the door for new conceptions of freedom, shared dreams of liberation, and a recognition that, to paraphrase Angela Davis, prisons are obsolete. The twenty-first century has ushered in a new generation of abolitionist organizations: Critical Resistance, Prison Moratorium Project, INCITE! (formerly known as INCITE! Women, Gender Non-Conforming, and Trans People of Color Against Violence,) Project NIA, the In Our Names Network, Dream Defenders, Black Youth Project 100, We Charge Genocide, and the #LetUs-Breathe Collective, to name a few.

I think about the late Kwame Somburu (previously Paul Boutelle) who, in 1968, called for abolishing the police while campaigning as the vice-presidential candidate on the Socialist Workers Party ticket. Harlem-born, Somburu grew up under police occupation. He drove a taxi for a living and became active in a number of anti-imperialist and Black nationalist organizations during the early '60s, including the Fair Play for Cuba Committee; the Freedom Now Party, an all-Black leftist political party; and Malcolm X's short-lived Organization of Afro-American Unity. Somburu's abolitionist vision called for free college education and medical care for all, a reduced work week with no corresponding reduction in pay, ending the Vietnam war and reinvesting those resources in "schools and hospitals" and "decent low-rent homes," nationalizing banks and major corporations and placing them "under the control of democratically elected workers' committees," and the "abolition of police." He proposed a public safety alternative that would entail electing representatives from communities to "replace troops and police."

I think about Shaka N'Zinga, an anarchist, political prisoner, and author of *A Disjointed Search for the Will to Live*. His capacity to see beauty and freedom in the midst of war is a characteristic shared by everyone Sonali interviewed. This passage says it all:

> There is a window in the building, inside the prison, that separates me from the living and acts as a beautiful vista into the life, the world, of which I am denied. Through this window I have a view of the carefree movements and activity of that day unfold before my longing eyes—done through the window of the prison that holds me; watching a honeybee alight upon a dandelion full of her needed honeymaking sustenance. A wonderful interaction between a wild cat and her litter of six kittens progress before my eyes, unhindered by the foulness of this blighted concentration camp that now inhibits my ability to be one in free and natural activity with them.[1]

For me, this is one of the most revolutionary passages in his book because it is about seeing the world as possibility from the place of confinement. Likewise, I can't help but think of Bomani Shakur, a.k.a. Keith LaMar, who sits on death row in the Southern Ohio Correctional Facility, convicted on completely trumped-up charges. Shakur is a poet, musician, artist, deep thinker, and critic who makes work that explores what it means to stay human in a dehumanizing system designed to kill. As I wrote in a letter to him:

> You carry this long tradition of resistance within you, evident in everything you do and say. It is there in your voice, your poetry, your music, your love of life and the people, and in your refusal to allow racist capitalist violence to define, limit, and destroy you. In the tradition of your ancestors, you refuse to be digested by this system; refuse to be refuse; refuse the bitter while holding fast to the Sweet. Each day of your life you prove the case for abolishing the death penalty and for abolishing prisons and jails altogether. As you put it, "It's them that's doing the ugly thing."

Abolitionists seek to replace death-dealing ugliness with life-sustaining beauty. It is an ancient idea "whose time has come," to quote Sonali. But much like the recurring dream that one day poor people will bring about a revolution and "take what's theirs," ideas must be realized in struggle. Those who rule will hold on to power by any means necessary, and the carceral state continues to be their most potent and effective weapon. They rely on fear and "copaganda" to convince us that replacing prisons and police with a humane, nonviolent, cage-free world committed to accountability, care, transformative justice, and redistribution will mean the end of civilization as we know it. But as these conversations reveal, this is precisely the point. Abolition. Revolution. Rebirth.

ROBIN D. G. KELLEY
Tunis, Tunisia
May 25, 2024

INTRODUCTION

"Every time I saw a white man, I was
afraid of being carried away."[2]
—HARRIET TUBMAN, abolitionist

The instinct to dial 911 in an emergency is embedded in the American psyche. However, Cat Brooks, an abolitionist organizer and community radio host, counters this. She notes, "Wide swaths of the Black and Brown community don't call the police because we know that when we dial that number, it is very rarely help that actually comes. What comes is an institution, or agents of an institution, who are trained to suppress, control, and subjugate, as opposed to help."

Studies consistently prove Brooks's assertion to be true, including a 2023 survey by the Movement for Black Lives (M4BL), which found that the majority of Black Americans are afraid of relying on police to help them in a crisis.[3] Meanwhile, the majority of white Americans are comfortable doing so. Gallup found that, from 2021 to 2023, confidence in policing among white Americans has hovered around seventy-five percent, despite the mass demonstrations against racist policing in 2020, in which many white Americans participated.[4]

The racial disparity over attitudes toward policing isn't the result of a bizarre built-in bias against authority among Black folks. The entire US system of criminal justice—from police patrolling and surveillance to the legal system of courts run by prosecutors and judges, culminating in incarceration—is sharply tilted against Black people. Black people don't trust the police because they face the existential threat of death or imprisonment during every interaction with a cop. Such conditions beg the question: has racial segregation truly ended?

In her powerful 2010 bestseller, *The New Jim Crow: Mass Incarceration in the Age of Colorblindness,* Michelle Alexander makes the case that no, it did not end. "Rather than rely on race, we use our criminal justice system to label people of color 'criminals' and then engage in all the practices we supposedly left behind," such as slavery and segregation, writes Alexander in her book.[5]

In 2016, filmmaker Ava DuVernay expanded on Alexander's work with her Oscar-nominated documentary *13th*, which draws a direct line from the end of slavery to the modern-day criminal justice system, making a powerful case that policing and incarceration are merely extensions of the original racist institutions in the United States.

There have been many compelling treatises in recent years written by US scholars proving the moral bankruptcy of racist policing. "[N]o aspect of national life—from the economy to education to electoral politics—has been untouched by the scale and scope of racialized policing and punishment," writes Khalil Gibran Muhammad, Professor of History, Race, and Public Policy at the Harvard Kennedy School, in his 2019 book, *The Condemnation of Blackness: Race, Crime, and the Making of Modern Urban America,* for example.[6]

Muhammad's book is part of a growing canon of work upending the notion that the American justice system is impartial. It's no wonder then that George Floyd's brutal murder at the hands of a police officer in Minneapolis sparked a raging inferno of anger among Americans of every racial background. According to one study, an estimated 15 to 26 million people marched in 8,700 racial justice protests that took place across the country between May 25 and July 31, 2020.[7]

However, merely calling attention to the racism embedded deeply within systems of policing is clearly not enough. Indeed, every year since Floyd's murder, police have progressively killed more people, with 1,347 people's lives snuffed out at the hands of law enforcement in 2023. That's more than 112 people killed per month, and ninety-six more than the previous year. Moreover, Black people are nearly 3 times more likely to be killed by police than white people.[8] Unless there is a serious intervention, we can expect the level of violence to continue to rise.

Similarly, it's not enough to simply denounce the perverse number of people who remain incarcerated. According to the Prison Policy Initiative, over the past half century the number of people held in state and federal prisons increased by an unimaginable 700 percent, with Black people being much more likely to remain trapped behind bars.[9]

When I think about the profound damage the carceral system inflicts on people, families, and communities, I cannot help but think of my friend, Darrell "Dortell" Williams, who has been imprisoned in California for more than thirty years. Although we've been friends for about two decades, we've never met in person. To me—a non-Black American who has not had to suffer the pain of seeing a family member incarcerated—his indefinite incarceration is symbolic of everything that is wrong with our current justice system.

"Prisons are a failed experiment that has no social, societal, or penological validation," writes Dortell in a letter to me from Chuckawalla Valley State Prison. For him, "the roots of crime" are "marginalization, poverty, and defunded zip codes," and "prisons themselves perpetuate these same ills." In using the word "defunded" to describe how vulnerable communities have been stripped of resources, Dortell references a solution to the violence of the system in which he remains trapped.

Alongside the protesters' message of "Black Lives Matter" in

2020, was the more esoteric "Defund the Police." Those latter three words hinted not only at the need to overhaul the American system of policing and prisons, but also at a reimagining of something entirely different as a means of enacting public safety.

Abolition Is an Evolving Idea

Minneapolis, where Floyd was killed, became the epicenter of the modern-day abolition movement in 2020. "We are actually building on decades of work from other organizers who have been doing abolition work and trying to move us towards a world in which abolition is possible,"[10] said Miski Noor, a leading organizer and activist with the Minneapolis-based Black Visions Collective. Noor cites the work of Ruth Wilson Gilmore and Andrea Ritchie as laying the groundwork for contemporary abolitionist organizing.

Indeed, there is a rich trove of abolitionist analyses available for those seeking to end policing as we know it. Angela Davis's 2003 book *Are Prisons Obsolete?* was a foundational publication that powerfully made the case for ending the American system of incarceration. "[L]arger prison populations led not to safer communities, but, rather, to even larger prison populations," writes Davis.[11]

In the late 1990s, Davis and Gilmore, together with scholar-activist Dylan Rodriguez, co-founded an abolitionist organization called Critical Resistance with an explicit focus on eradicating prisons, the carceral end point of policing. At around the same time, the Los Angeles Police Department (LAPD) became embroiled in a scandal of epic proportions that made national headlines.

Starting in the 2000s, I interviewed Gilmore, Rodriguez, and other prison abolitionists on my daily drive-time radio program, airing on a community station based in Los Angeles called KPFK Pacifica Radio. During that period, I also covered street actions in downtown LA. I witnessed Angelinos protest the ugly corruption at the heart of the LAPD, particularly its Rampart Division. Hundreds of police officers were implicated in abusive and corrupt practices, which led to untold numbers of wrongful convictions.

Despite evidence of systemic failures, imagining a world without prisons—let alone police—was considered far more radical at that time than it is today. However, thanks to the last few decades of dogged work from largely Black activists and academics such as Gilmore and Noor, abolition has become a far more acceptable idea.

In 2019, the *New York Times* printed an extensive profile of Gilmore as a prison abolitionist.[12] In 2021, the *New Yorker* published Keeanga-Yamahtta Taylor's powerful piece titled "The Emerging Movement for Police and Prison Abolition."[13] And in 2022, *Harper's Bazaar* conducted an in-depth interview with Angela Davis and Gina Dent about their book, *Abolition. Feminism. Now.*[14]

It seems abolition is an idea whose time has come. This book is intended to connect the abolitionist work done in the 2000s and 2010s to the resurgence of interest in abolitionism since the 2020 uprising for racial justice. The wheels of abolition are already in motion. Many of those leading the change tell their stories here.

Enforcing and Preserving Racial Capitalism

"The United States is unlike any other place on the planet," Gilmore said to me in a 2011 interview, "and the states that have the worst prison systems are also the ones that have the biggest gaps between rich and poor." She added, "We as Americans have got to get serious about thinking of the ways that people are abandoned—we have immigrants locked up, people of color locked up, mentally ill people locked up, people with addictions locked up—and reconsider how it is that we *should* be in this world."[15]

She deepened this analysis in a conversation we had in 2023, on which Chapter Two of this book is based. "Abolition," says Gilmore, "lets us look at how people are struggling and understand the organized abandonment that characterizes so much of everyday life under capitalism."

Our criminal justice system is deeply intertwined with our economic system. It's no coincidence that the same society that embraces racist policing and imprisonment is also one where people of color, and Black people in particular, remain deeply disadvantaged compared to white people.[16] The system born from white supremacist ideals that enriched white enslavers and their progeny has largely maintained its socio-economic hierarchy in the modern world. And therefore, as Andrea Ritchie says in Chapter One, "What police are charged with doing is maintaining the existing social order." They are the "muscle of racial capitalism."

For decades, politicians have responded to the violence of policing by assuming it was a flaw that needed fixing, a few "bad apples" that needed expunging. But, as abolitionist attorney Noelle Hanrahan says in Chapter Four, "the system is designed to function exactly as it was planned. It is not broken. It is doing a service for the ruling class, the capitalist class, those who want to manage people who are demanding food, work, and bread, and humanity."

Those who believe the police could be a force for good have backed many tiny (and expensive) tweaks to law enforcement. They respond to its inherent abusiveness with stricter protocols for physical interactions, body cameras, or diversity training. Such tweaks have not only preserved policing but relegitimized it again and again. "There is a kind of stubborn persistence, a stubborn loyalty to those things as forms of power that actually provide social work," says Dylan Rodriguez in Chapter Three. He calls out the "almost religious loyalty" to policing as an "anti-Black and colonial power, as that which gives order to the world."

City budgets tell the story of such loyalties in cold hard numbers, as lawmakers direct jaw-dropping portions of tax revenue into their local police departments. This leaves public goods—including libraries, afterschool programs, job training, public transportation, and the like—to fight over the crumbs.

For example, according to the Vera Institute of Justice, the portion of the city budget spent on policing is twenty-six percent in Baltimore, Maryland; thirty-four percent in Wilmington, Delaware; thirty-seven percent in Chicago, Illinois; thirty-six percent in Houston, Texas; forty-one percent in Phoenix, Arizona; and a whopping sixty-four percent in Billings, Montana.[17] In attempting to reform police—which has turned out to be an exercise in futility—city and state officials have poured yet more public resources into systems designed to maintain racial injustice from their inception.

It's not just police departments that are sucking up our precious tax dollars. Courts, jails, and prisons also extract resources at the expense of public safety and well-being. Ivette Alé-Ferlito, cofounder of the abolitionist organization La Defensa, calls courts "a line of production for incarceration" in Chapter Eight. They add that "the budgets for the judiciary have been climbing for the last twenty years, and the increases in judicial spending are reflected in the expansion of our criminal legal system and mass incarceration."

This vastly expensive and patently anti-Black system of oppression preserves economic hierarchies along racial lines and has stubbornly persisted at the center of American civilization. It is, at its core, deeply *uncivilized*. So, what do we do about it?

Defund the Police = Invest/Divest = Care Not Cops = Care First, Jails Last

It is incumbent on governments to equalize wealth distribution. But the very resources that could do so via things like housing assistance, job training, small business subsidies and grants, and free college are diverted into funding the armed enforcers of inequality. Given this, the call to "Defund the Police" makes profound sense. However, liberal politicians and corporate media pundits, while embracing "Black Lives Matter" in 2020, rejected the idea behind the accompanying slogan of "Defund the Police,"[18] and maintained the big lie that there is no alternative to police, prisons, and the entire criminal justice system.

What if they—what if *we*—instead poured resources into those institutions that have actually been proven to promote public safety and well-being? Moving money out of policing, courts, and prisons and into public services is a straightforward idea, which the slogan "Defund the Police" attempts to capture. The same idea has been expressed in various other, perhaps less provocative, formations, such as "Invest/Divest," "Care, Not Cops," and "Care First, Jails Last."

Regardless of the phrasing, the sentiment is the same: let's invest resources into the things that keep us safe rather than policing. Such thinking has informed discussions around budgetary processes in various cities where abolitionists have been active. In Chapter Nine, longtime Black Lives Matter activist and California State University, Los Angeles professor Melina Abdullah lays out how cities can be pushed to enact participatory budgeting processes so that city residents can decide how to spend their tax dollars. By surveying those who are made aware of the extent of city police budgets, she finds that "people, regardless of political persuasion, tend to lean towards defunding the police." She acknowledges that "simply having a participatory budgeting process is not abolition," but "it pulls people in, so they begin to ask questions about why do we spend money here and not there?"

Abolition may feel too big and too complicated to achieve. In Chapter Five, Reina Sultan, who helped build the website 8toabolition.com in the summer of 2020 when interest in such ideas spiked, writes "It's hard to imagine change when you've only known this way of living." But it's not really that complicated. Sultan articulates a handful of clear steps to achieving abolition, starting with "Defund the Police," and ending with "Invest in Care, Not Cops." The steps are a distillation of ideas articulated and put into practice in various ways and at various times by abolitionist activists and public intellectuals.

The idea of investing in community care over policing is popular, and why not? The M4BL survey conducted in 2023 found that "86% of Black people support creating a new agency of first responders who specialize in de-escalating violence and providing mental health support and other social services that would take over these responsibilities from police."[19] Well-funded social structures supporting public health and education; quality employment; living wages; and access to fair housing, clean air, and fresh, healthy food could diminish, if not entirely erase, the need for a criminal justice system.

Such projects are already underway in many US cities. As Eunisses Hernandez, the young abolitionist organizer who became an LA city councilmember, says in Chapter 7, "We have had a lot of success in moving money out of the carceral system into community, in moving money that was destined for jail construction into access to housing and care."

Hernandez coauthored Measure J, a citywide ballot measure passed in November 2020 which directs a chunk of LA's budget into nonpolice public safety programs. *The LA Times* Editorial board called Measure J "the nation's most lasting and consequential criminal justice reform strategy to arise from the social movements of 2020."[20]

Black Futures and the Promise of a Multiracial Democracy

Cat Brooks says, "A world without police doesn't mean a world without accountability. It means that what we're doing right now actually doesn't create safety for anyone." Abolishing slavery and segregation were not enough to end the scourge of virulent racism infecting the heart and soul of the United States. If policing and prisons are merely extensions of slavery and Jim Crow segregation, then the original project of slavery's abolition is incomplete.

The necessary next phase of abolition, then, is to eradicate policing, prisons, and the courts, while simultaneously building up structures that actually promote community safety and creating a future where a multiracial democracy can thrive. We can think of this as a grand unifying theory of abolition.

Turning that theory into practice is not an impractical prospect at all. Black women are at the forefront of realizing abolitionist ideals. Alongside Indigenous Americans, Black women in the US have faced the worst forms of violence and marginalization, historically and in the present day.[21] They have also led the most inspiring struggles for freedom and originated the most powerful and radical analyses of what is necessary for collective liberation. It is the reason why I, as a non-Black person of color, have taken my lead from Black women visionaries and why the majority of the interview subjects in this book are Black women.

In Chapter Twelve, Alicia Garza, one of three Black women who popularized the phrase "Black Lives Matter," says "When we think about laws and policies that impact our lives, most of the time our communities are not involved in the development of those processes, but we certainly are impacted by them." To that end, Garza, who founded the Black Futures Lab says, "We want to change that equation. We think that Black communities deserve to be the people who are making the rules, and changing the rules, that are shaping our lives every single day."

This book, although by no means comprehensive, is a compilation of the ideas and views of twelve movement leaders, rule changers, and culture shapers who envision a future where both the unequal socio-economic order and the enforcers of that inequality are obsolete.

On the other side of abolition lies a beautiful world where quality education and libraries, food and housing, physical and mental healthcare, satisfying work, and good pay, are not just theoretical rights, but are available to all. It is a world where we can all thrive, especially those among us who have been historically excluded from the largesse of American wealth.

It's never too early to begin visualizing and actualizing that future. Many are doing just that. In Chapter Eleven, acclaimed food justice organizer and farmer Leah Penniman links abolitionist ideals of rebuilding new worlds to land, food, and farming, saying that "the food system is essentially incarcerated in corporate racial capitalism" and that the severing of Black and Brown people's ties to the land goes hand in hand with policing and mass incarceration. Conversely, freeing land from corporate control, says Penniman, is central to freeing people from prisons and policing.

And finally, in Chapter Twelve, feminist abolitionist Gina Dent reminds us that "the carceral system is naturalized for us," and that "we are taught over and over again that we need to rely on it." Consequently, "that's the only thing we can imagine." Dent calls for a wholesale cultural transformation of the individualist mindsets and behaviors that drive incarceration, down to our personal interactions with one another.

This book is intended to weave the many disparate threads of abolitionist theory and practice into a coherent tapestry that can guide us into the future, applying a necessary sense of urgency. After all, the lives and dignity of our fellow human beings—like my friend Dortell Williams—are at stake. Some have survived the horrors of police abuse and incarceration. Far too many remain caged, suffering daily dehumanization. Many live in fear. Far too many have died already. Many more will be killed.

We have the power and the responsibility to transform this system.

"[I]t should be remembered that the ancestors of many of today's most ardent liberals could not have imagined life without slavery, life without lynching, or life without segregation," says Angela Davis in *Are Prisons Obsolete?*[22] The same historical throughline that connects chattel slavery to the contemporary system of policing and mass incarceration extends to abolition. Those who imagined a slavery-free future lifted the nation up to the path to freedom. Modern-day abolitionists are walking that same path in order to finish the task their ancestors began.

I

ANDREA RITCHIE

RACIAL CAPITALISM REQUIRES POLICING

The roots of abolition lie in a critique of how policing and punishment are deployed in the service of maintaining and bolstering existing power relations. Andrea J. Ritchie, a nationally recognized expert on policing and criminalization, has an intimate understanding of this relationship.

A writer, organizer, researcher, and policy advocate, Ritchie has litigated and resisted police practices in New York City. She has collaborated with and supported organizers across the United States. She has also written extensively on the intersections of criminalization, race, gender, sexuality, and policing. She is a cofounder of the In Our Names Network, a coalition of more than twenty organizations working to end police violence against Black women, girls, trans and gender nonconforming people. Together with Mariame Kaba, she also cofounded Interrupting Criminalization, an initiative that challenges the carceral state. Ritchie and Kaba cowrote *No More Police: A Case for Abolition.*

During my conversation with her in August 2022, Ritchie explained how racial capitalism requires policing to enforce the existing order in an unequal society, how the police foster violence rather than public safety, and how communities across the US are pushing to defund law enforcement.

* * *

SONALI KOLHATKAR: The idea to "defund the police" was not new in 2020; it was only new to the mainstream press and politicians. We know that the idea of defunding the police goes back a few years, but the idea of abolishing the carceral state goes back decades, right?

ANDREA RITCHIE: Absolutely. I certainly think that the notion of defunding police gained a great deal more traction over the last couple of years, but it is something that can be traced back much further.

For instance, Angela Davis—a leading Black feminist abolitionist who's inspired both Mariame Kaba and me in this work—traces, in some ways, the conversation back to W.E.B. Du Bois. In his book *Black Reconstruction in America*, Du Bois calls for an "abolition democracy," which undoes the vestiges of slavery and redistributes wealth, resources, and power in such a way as to rectify the legacy of slavery, correct it, heal from it, and transform it in our society.

In many ways, the call to defund police grows from that vision. It's a call to take resources, power, and legitimacy away from institutions rooted in anti-Blackness, in racial capitalism, and death making: policing, punishment, surveillance, and exile. It's a call to reinvest in the commons, a society built around the notion of the common good, and everyone's needs being met.

I think that the focus on police and prisons as part of that movement came about in the 1990s, as more and more funding was being taken—stolen—from education, social programs, common goods, social services, public parks, libraries, etc., and poured increasingly into policing, prisons, and immigration enforcement. And as that trend has skyrocketed, so has resistance to it, which has spread across the country.

KOLHATKAR: So, when the rallying cry of "defund the police" in 2020 was met with opposition, that was a presidential election year. We had then-candidate Joe Biden saying he was not in favor of defunding police. Other establishment politicians also drew a line, saying, "Yes, we're all for racial justice, yes, Black Lives Matter, but certainly we don't want to defund the police." And then, in May 2022, we saw a horrifying example of how police don't equal safety with the elementary school shooting in Uvalde, Texas when police failed to protect children from a mass shooter. Was that a turning point for this notion that police are central to public safety when police did nothing for over an hour as children were being shot?

RITCHIE: The question we have to ask ourselves is, "What is the moment when you first began to question the violence of policing?" And there have been so many moments. Uvalde was a horrifying one that certainly drew a lot of people into the conversation who maybe had been hesitant to enter it before. And there have been many more, and there are many more every single day. Some gain more national traction and prominence than others.

Fewer than half the survivors of gender-based violence turn to the police because of the violence and criminalization that police perpetrate, and also because police fail to prevent, interrupt, or heal from violence. It's an ongoing horror that more than half of survivors of violence aren't able or willing to avail themselves of the thing that is increasingly getting the resources to address the harms they're experiencing. That's sort of a quiet Uvalde, right?

Then, there are the daily spectacular forms of violence, some of which gain national attention, which keep making the case for folks that policing has failed.

So, I invite folks to think about the moment in which, for them, the violence of policing and its equation with public safety was ruptured. And then let's think about what that rupture makes possible in terms of the imagination of what could be, and in creating safer, more just, thriving, and sustainable communities.

And the point you make about politicians is really important, because "defund the police" is a very concrete demand that asks them to put their money where their mouth is. It's a demand that asks them to go beyond mouthing platitudes while wearing Kente cloth to actually making material change that will end the violence—the anti-Black violence, the anti-Indigenous, the anti-migrant, the settler-colonial racial capitalist violence—that is policing. Defunding the police also demands that politicians shift resources in ways that undermine the over-accumulation of wealth and promote more equitable distributions of resources. So, of course, they don't want to do that, and that's why there's been such a powerful and intense backlash against the demand, which, I would argue, is a demonstration of its power.

KOLHATKAR: Those who defend police funding might admit that police are often violating their own ideals, that they are often the perpetrators of violence. But their solution is to *reform* the police. We've seen years of reform policies, like outfitting cops with body cameras and creating citizen commissions that oversee police. Where do you stand on the idea of reforming the police instead of defunding it?

RITCHIE: Mariame Kaba always invites us to write the word reform in a hyphenated way, *re-form*, because that's what you're doing. You're *re-forming* the same thing into a new shape with the same purpose.

Another thing we did at Interrupting Criminalization—which was one brilliant idea of thousands that came out of Mariame's head—was to create a series of posters in which we, and other scholars and organizers, define policing in one sentence. Because, at the core, what reformists misapprehend is what police are. They're not broken. They're not rogue. They're not in need of a policy reform or a new rule or more intense discipline or more intense regulation through civil litigation. They're not violating their own ideals. They're doing exactly what they were set up to do, and they're doing it very well.

Police are clear that the rules don't apply to them. What they are charged with doing is maintaining the existing social order. Politicians give them free rein to use untold violence, criminalization, suffering, and pain and punishment in order to do that. As Alyxandra Goodwin, formerly of the Action Center on Race and the Economy, says, "police are the muscle of racial capitalism." Police are violence, not safety. You can't reform something that's doing exactly what it was meant to do. If you need further proof of that, you can look to the last century of attempts to minimize the harms of policing: make it do what we hope it could do while taking away its more harmful aspects. Each attempt has failed.

The attempts sometimes take technological forms. We often think, *oh, tech will save us*—like body cameras or tasers—but we find the same patterns being perpetuated. And that, to us, provides clear evidence of what policing is. We can't keep throwing good money away trying to recuperate a bad institution that has been death making since its inception.

KOLHATKAR: When the mass racial justice protests happened in 2020 in the wake of George Floyd's killing in Minneapolis, the Minneapolis City Council started to consider the demand to defund the police. And if you just read the mainstream press or the right-wing press, Minneapolis did defund its police. What actually happened?

RITCHIE: The stories being told about our work and what's happening are manipulated to serve the relegitimization of policing. We have witnessed one of the greatest crises of legitimacy for policing in the United States in decades, and there has been a swift, powerful, and ongoing backlash fueled by the mainstream media. This has occurred in much the same way that Ida B. Wells described how mainstream media were accomplices to lynching.

There's a way in which mainstream media attempt to recuperate police, blame violence in our communities not on lack of things that we need to survive, but instead on individuals and on low police morale, and on the absence of police in some way. We need to deconstruct those narratives.

I think the story of Minneapolis is central to this, and it didn't start on May 25, 2020. Key organizations at the epicenter of that uprising had succeeded in defunding the police department by over a million dollars in 2018. The mayor there eventually came back and re-funded it.

This was an ongoing struggle in the city. It wasn't just that a demand came out of a moment. It came out of struggle, organizing, political education, and political analysis around what the impact of reform had been in Minneapolis.

Minneapolis police had adopted the vast majority of the gold standard reforms, the best practices promoted by the Department of Justice and everyone else. Derek Chauvin had been trained not to do exactly what he did when he kneeled on George Floyd's neck for nine minutes. Minneapolis police had all the policies and training, and they still killed Floyd.

The movement to defund the police in Minneapolis was seeded by many years of organizing, political education, and analysis. What's happened in Minneapolis has been really beautiful; people have been engaging community members through surveys, through People's Movement Assemblies, and through ongoing conversations to determine what people need to really feel safe.

There have been many experiments and practices. There are groups like Relationships Evolving Possibilities, the Powderhorn Safety Collective, and Little Earth Protectors who are really thinking about and practicing what it looks like to create safety without police. A lot of their work is documented by One Million Experiments if folks want to check it out.

And then there's the People's Movement Assembly. Black Visions put out a report on a series of conversations that happened in 2020, and they went back for a budget fight in 2021. They also fought for a ballot initiative that would have unshackled the city from a mandatory level of police funding in place since 1961 when a police union organized to keep cops' jobs during an earlier crisis of legitimacy.

There's been much work happening on the ground in ways that are less visible than the burning of the Third Precinct, but certainly equally revolutionary in the sense that they're really engaging people in conversation in Minneapolis about what safety looks like. The city council has come and gone with the headlines in some respects. Some folks have stayed in the struggle, others have sort of blown with the political winds. But we know that's how organizing works, and the key to organizing is building power to make it impossible for people to ignore your demands. We did that in 2020, and people are continuing to do that across the country.

KOLHATKAR: Are there other cities in the country where you see activists successfully chipping away at the funding that police, the carceral state, and the prison system get, and putting that into the things that foster public safety and funding for the things that we actually need? Are there success stories at the micro level that we can look to as we imagine a world without police?

RITCHIE: There are too many to chronicle, and you can find out more about all of them at DefundPolice.org, which is a site that gathers information from cities and towns and locations across the country doing this work.

I will say that the biggest success is that cities and communities across the country engaged in similar conversations to the ones that Black Visions and Reclaim the Block and many other groups in Minneapolis engaged in around what safety looks like in communities. Black Nashville Assembly, Jackson People's Assembly, and many other groups across the country engaged in community conversations about what safety requires that didn't necessarily make headlines.

Some cities and organizers were successful in commandeering, taking over, and mobilizing city-announced public safety task forces to build out recommendations that would pour resources into meeting the needs of people and their communities. This happened in Austin, Texas; in Oakland, California; and in Durham, North Carolina, for instance. And in all of those cities, organizers are still very much contending for power around implementation of those recommendations, funding of those initiatives, etc., with varying degrees of success.

There has been success across the board. Prior to 2020, city policymakers felt empowered to write a blank check to the cops whenever they came and demanded money. Now, they feel like they have to justify what they're doing, because they know that the organizers are going to come for them. There are billboards up in Los Angeles and Milwaukee today that talk about how much money is going to the police and other things. That wasn't something they had to contend with before, and that's the power that we've built. So that's really important. There are many ways that people are continuing this work that are reflected in Interrupting Criminalization's January 2023 publication *The Struggle Continues.*

I do want to lift up the work being done in Seattle, which gets too little attention. They're the only city that defunded their police department two years in a row, in 2020 and 2021,[23] and that secured millions of dollars for community safety projects and millions more for a participatory budgeting process. A year later, the city was dragging its feet on implementing that.

KOLHATKAR: When you say "defund," you mean taking some money out of the police budget, not closing down the police department, right?

RITCHIE: They have taken significant amounts of money out of the police budget. They've also taken 911 operators out of the police purview. They have taken some other functions out of the police department. Minneapolis did the same, taking 911 out of the police department, which makes more things possible.

If the people answering the phone aren't the police, they might offer you some options that aren't the police and might be safer and actually meet your needs.

I think Atlanta has been very successful in doing that. The Policing Alternatives and Diversion Initiative has now created an option with 311 that you can call nonpolice responders: community responders who are going to offer folks a range of options rather than a cage. There are places everywhere where these things are happening.

KOLHATKAR: Denver, Colorado has a really interesting alternative to calling the police, right?

RITCHIE: What's interesting about Denver—and this is true across the country—is that when the cops see something that looks like it's successful or is going to be successful in taking away some of their power or resources, they will set up a competing program. In Denver, because 911 was taken out of the police department, they conscripted the 911 operators to make sure they got the calls for their co-response program, as opposed to the nonpolice community response program.

Interrupting Criminalization documented that in a report called "Defund the Police—Invest in Community Care" based on conversations with local organizers. We also recently put out a report gathering lessons from two years of communities fighting for community response programs: *Building Coordinated Crisis Response*. We also need to pay attention to the fact that the more successful we are, the more viciously the police are going to fight back. They will use fearmongering narratives, literally stealing calls from people. They will also undermine violence-interruption programs by fomenting violence, not answering calls for help, and then blaming "defund."

And they're continuing to criminalize poverty. Seattle police have been doing almost daily sweeps of unhoused people and then claiming that they don't have the resources to answer domestic violence calls.

KOLHATKAR: Let's focus on the notion of racial capitalism, which I think is central to this topic. The word "defund" itself gets to the heart of that: taking money away from police and putting it back into the things that foster public safety so that we don't need police. Because currently, as it stands, we have a society where wealth keeps flowing upwards, and to quell the unrest among the masses, police are deemed "necessary." That is an analysis that we almost never get in the mainstream media where you might get critiques of capitalism, and you might get critiques of police, but you rarely get critiques that connect the two.

RITCHIE: I am a student of Ruth Wilson Gilmore, Angela Davis, Robin D. G. Kelley, and so many people who have made those clear connections. They are definitely my touchstones, among others. And many scholars and organizers in Critical Resistance and INCITE! have historically made those connections. The Black Panthers made those connections. They're also part of the origin story of "defund" demands. So are incarcerated people who, in the 1970s, were calling for the abolition of the judicial-prison-parole-industrial complex.

And so, we have to learn from people who are directly targeted by racial capitalism. We have to learn from Angela Davis who says that criminalization and prisons are designed to hide the effects of racial capitalism. We have to learn from Ruth Wilson Gilmore who says capitalism is consistently trying to resolve crises of its own creation, and criminalization is one of the primary ways that it does so.

The current manifestation of racial capitalism—neoliberalism—is essentially the opposite of "defund the police," right? Neoliberalism is defunding education, social services, public housing, libraries, hospitals, health care, public goods of any kind, including resources for people in need. It diverts those funds to capital and then criminalizes people who are trying to survive under increasingly desperate conditions. This is not acceptable.

We must refund the commons. And that's what the demand to defund the police is: a collective effort to take money away from death-giving institutions and redirect them into life-giving institutions. Part of our strategy is to accomplish this in ways that do not reenact and reaffirm policing in new ways, in the ways that social welfare programs, social work, or public health and medical treatment can and often do.

Abolition is really about reimagining: what forms of society, sociology, political economy, and governance can we create to enact our liberation dreams so that everyone has everything that they need to reach their highest human potential?

What's going to make that possible? Defunding the police is definitely a necessary step. It's certainly not the last, but it's a clear step in that direction. And that, I think, is the power of the demand.

2

RUTH WILSON GILMORE

FREEDOM IS A PLACE

For more than thirty years, Ruth Wilson Gilmore has created scholarship on an idea once considered radical: society does not need to abandon people and secure that abandonment with organized violence. This led her to scholarship on, among other things, the analysis of prisons toward the goal of their abolition, imagining abolition as the greater goal—which is to change everything. Now, with greater attention being paid to how people of color—and Black people in particular—are disproportionately targeted by the criminal justice system and prison industrial complex, Gilmore's ideas are being validated, even by the likes of the *New York Times*, which published a lengthy feature about her in 2019, taking seriously an issue the paper has historically dismissed.

Gilmore is a professor of Earth and Environmental Sciences and American Studies, and director of the Center for Place, Culture and Politics at the City University of New York Graduate Center. She cofounded several grassroots organizations, including the California Prison Moratorium Project, Critical Resistance, and the Central California Environmental Justice Network. She is the author of two books, including *Abolition Geography: Essays Towards Liberation*, which is based on her numerous lectures and papers spanning several decades.

In this conversation, which took place in January 2023, Gilmore frames the idea of abolition within geography, economy, and the academy.

❋ ❋ ❋

SONALI KOLHATKAR: You paint your ideas of decarceration around the "geography of abolition." What does that mean, exactly?

RUTH WILSON GILMORE: Well, you know, the title of my book isn't *The Geography of Abolition*. It's *Abolition Geography*. And I put the words together, in that order, to make a peculiar kind of point—we create the conditions for our everyday lives by organizing ourselves, materials, and environmental resources. And, in putting those things together—sometimes institutionally as states or corporations or communities or unions, and sometimes in more free-flowing ways, let's say, how mutual aid societies work—what we're doing is creating a place. Whether that place is small or big makes no difference. And those places can become abolition geographies. So that's why "abolition" goes in front of "geography" rather than after a preposition.

KOLHATKAR: So, thinking about space, is that a way to visualize, in real terms, what abolition could look like, because otherwise it might seem abstract?

GILMORE: That is exactly right. That's a really good way of putting it. For many people, when they first encounter this idea that seems so far-fetched—that we might abolish institutions of organized violence, such as police and prisons—they imagine some kind of void, something that isn't, rather than all of the things that must be for that imagination to come into reality. And for us to make reality, we have to—and I'm going to repeat myself already—we have to make places. There is no social life that is not spatial life. There is no kind of dream of a better future that isn't also a dream of organizing ourselves with one another and the environments in particular places, wherever they might be.

So, while most of my political experience over the last thirty years has been based in California, it's not exclusively there. The kind of thinking that I and others have been trying to develop in close collaboration with, and as, organizers, is emerging in different places around the planet, all propelled by different kinds of urgencies.

KOLHATKAR: You're an academic. And I suppose it's no surprise that the university ends up being a place of origin for many freedom movements around the world, for example in places like Iran and Latin America where you see a lot of student-led movements. Do you see the academy as a place of power where the intellectual agenda for society can get set?

GILMORE: That's correct. And, you know, thinking with you along this trail, one thing that we can dwell on briefly is that making curricular decisions is obviously a form of power. It shapes what happens in classrooms and why, or, to raise those questions that you just cited: who studies, who teaches, who learns what, and to what end?

We can do that in a number of ways. We can do it in sort of noisy ways, trying to demand change from the top. Or we can do it somewhat more quietly in the context of classrooms.

I know that my colleagues in Florida, who are figuring out how to do these things, continue to do what they've been doing quietly in classrooms. And anybody who's listening in from the "Florida thought police" will probably never figure out the multiple ways that people figure out how to teach.

KOLHATKAR: And you cite Florida because that seems to be the epicenter of attacks on things like critical race theory by Governor Ron DeSantis?

GILMORE: Exactly. And, of course, although Florida's leading the way, plenty of other states and school districts are rapidly following. So, one of the ways that people struggle to figure out how to fight in the context of so much fascist and proto-fascist repression is sometimes to make huge declamations, which are correct, and other times, as I said earlier, to work more quietly and persistently and in collaboration with as many other people as possible.

It's true as well that universities and colleges in the United States are all going through a very, very long sea change. In the time that I was coming of age in the middle of the twentiethcentury, the opportunities for higher education were expanding significantly and dramatically. The number of seats within higher education grew every year. So, while the desegregation of postsecondary education by both race and gender shifted dramatically in that time, it's also true that the entire size of universities grew quite dramatically from the 1950s until the early 1980s.

During that time, school was not exactly free, but even private schools were, relatively speaking, affordable, because of how prices were set, how financial aid works, how debt was a very small—if present at all—aspect of how individuals and families paid for school, and so forth. But starting in the very late 1970s and early 1980s, the price of postsecondary education took off, hand in hand with a rise in the availability of student loans, which had been a very small component of federal financial aid up until the late 1970s. So, all of this weight of debt has had a conservatizing effect on people for the obvious reason.

Debt always makes people more conservative, whether your debt is to pay your credit card, house mortgage, car note, or to pay your school debt, or the other kinds of debts that people have. Debt is a frightening thing, and it makes people somewhat more conservative, until and unless they figure out—as the hundreds of thousands of people who have been active in the Debt Collective in recent years have learned—that if they band together, then instead of becoming more individualized and conservative, what people can do is agitate nonstop for relief from such debt.

It might be news to many people that the Debt Collective, which has a very high profile for being a leading voice against the debilitating consequences of student debt, is equally committed to relieving people of medical debt. And if we had time, I would discuss the debilitating features of certain kinds of debt at various scales, including the structural adjustment imposed on places throughout the Global South but also, for example, the City of New York in the 1970s.

KOLHATKAR: What can abolition geography look like outside of the academy, in society, to thwart white supremacy? How can we envision an abolition geography that is anti-racist?

GILMORE: A way to think about it through the lens of class war. We can learn about class war by reading people like Stuart Hall—one of my great mentors and influences—very carefully. Class war is lived through the modalities of race, nation, national origin, sexuality, and gender. All of those different categories of existence, which we all invoke all the time, together shape class.

I don't like the word "intersection" very much, but I think what people who find Kimberlé Crenshaw's idea of intersectionality useful are trying to say is that there are multiple interactions that shape experience. They don't necessarily, though, create a specificity of experience that is wholly separate from the experiences of people whose categorical aspects come together in other ways.

So, the large context for abolition geography is necessarily racial capitalism. And if it is necessarily racial capitalism, it is also, as you were saying earlier, the carceral state, or states in general.

Now, I'm not anti-state. I'm not an anarchist. I have not concluded yet—and I'm almost seventy-four years old—that something called the state must at all times be more against me than for me. I think that we need big things like transportation, clean water, and adequate housing. And I believe in education and parks and art and health care. And I haven't been convinced that these are things that we can make through some kind of mutual aid self-sufficiency. But my views are open for us to debate.

Where abolition comes in is in our ability to understand the specificities of class war as we look around the world. Even setting aside the experiences of people who do not live in white supremacist, settler colonial states—because most people on the planet don't—class war is as vibrant and devastating in those places as it is in the US or Canada or Australia or South Africa.

So, what then, I ask myself, does abolition bring to a general concern about the question of class war and the underlying question of how we understand class composition?

Many people's definition of class has been outdated for as long as they've written about it. Let us say when Marx was still alive and the Paris Commune had, quite successfully, even for a limited period, taken over a good deal of that city, one could not say something crisp and clear about what the class that composed that uprising and successful takeover looked like.

Or, if we look around the world as it transformed in the 20th century into the USSR or the People's Republic of China and other places, we see that the class composition of those revolutionary societies was not dominated by an industrialized proletariat. It was really mixed. It was proletarians and peasants and all kinds of people in between. And yet the revolutionary fervor arose from the ground up, due to how people connected their senses of vulnerability with their demands for protection and opportunity.

And that's where we are, I think, in the current moment. Abolition compels us to look at how people are struggling, understand the organized abandonment that characterizes so much of everyday life under capitalism, and understand that such organized abandonment is maintained, bordered, and boundaried by the forces of organized violence. We can see that most explicitly in prison and police. It's not only there, but that's where we see it most explicitly.

Taking that wider view through the lens of abolition, we can see that in any number of circumstances in which people are actually struggling, the contours of class will not necessarily reflect categorically something called the industrial proletariat. What we will see are people who are struggling because of the organization of capitalist accumulation, whose need to control land, to have housing, to have food, to have water, to move around, to stay put, is shaped by the forces of organized violence. Abolition says clearly that this is a central struggle in all class war.

KOLHATKAR: So then would it be safe to say that abolition of prisons does not, and cannot, happen in isolation because if we want to see an end of the prison state, we have to understand how deeply it is a part of our racial capitalist system? And that, in order to envision a world without prisons, we need to envision an entirely different world altogether?

GILMORE: That is exactly right. Some people may say, "Oh, that's so unrealistic, envisioning an entirely different world!"

I say, "How often do you connect with people through a computer screen?" The world we are in now is entirely different from the world I was born into and the one our parents were born into.

Imagining the impossible is what people in the struggle for

liberation do and have been doing. That's what it is. And there are all different kinds of actions and energies that come together to realize their struggle.

I'll give an example from a recent experience that I had. My partner, Craig Gilmore, and I were in South Africa for three weeks in 2022, from the end of November through the middle of December. We had been invited there by some comrades. Our hosts were members of the University of the Western Cape in Cape Town; an organization called The Forge in Johannesburg; and the Shack Dwellers' organization Abahlali baseMjondolo which is kind of dotted around South Africa, centered most strongly in Durban.

The people who are active and organized in Abahlali are people who, in the desperation of needing a place to live—this is basic, a place to live—have collectively occupied land and built houses. They have used every possible means to defend the houses, including legal methods such as appeals to the constitution and other methods, even as the forces of organized violence—including the central state police, provincial police, metropolitan police, private security, eviction units, and so forth—are constantly destroying the communities the people have built.

Abahlali has been around for fifteen or sixteen years now. We had the opportunity to visit several of the different settlements dotted around the country, meet with leadership, and talk to people. It was quite astonishing.

What we saw, of course, in these people building socialism from the ground up was people realizing the impossible. There's nothing utopian about the everyday lives of people in these communities, and yet these were places where people feel a lot of hope and energy and possibility because of what they have accomplished together.

Have they exited the state? No. Instead, they are demanding

that the state—whether it's the municipal or provincial or central government—provide water and sanitation and all of the other things that the state should provide. So, it's not as though they've built a self-sustaining community that doesn't need running water and electricity. They need those things, and what has happened in some cases is that people have successfully gotten the infrastructural support that any residential community needs by working together in building and maintaining their communities. At their hearts, these are fights over urban space: land and dignity.

If we turn our sights to Brazil—somewhere I haven't been yet—we see that the Landless Workers' Movement (MST) is doing similar kinds of work. The Abahlali and the MST are in conversation with one another in a really beautiful and strongly internationalist demonstration of solidarity. This is happening in other places as well.

These are examples of abolition geography. They're examples of people not only doing anti-racist work by polemicizing about racism—which is necessary when it's necessary—but by making something. By making and doing things. And quite often some of that possibility doesn't even seem realizable until, for example, artists have helped people open their imaginations to what can be done.

And I don't mean our artists making up a kind of science-fiction fable that then ordinary people realize, but just the way that art opens your mind and heart to—even if you can't quite explain them—the possibilities for different configurations of human and resource interaction.

KOLHATKAR: They call it world building these days.

GILMORE: World building! That's even better.

KOLHATKAR: It seems as though many white, leftist, anti-capitalist thinkers don't explicitly connect the dismantling of the criminal justice system with the dismantling of capitalism. Can abolition be a portal to a postcapitalist world?

GILMORE: It has to be a portal to a postcapitalist world, as I explained earlier. I can't explain why some white, leftist, anti-capitalist thinkers imagine police-state socialism is a necessary portal. I'd also like to note that while white leftists can be a problem, abolition is not an anti-white movement any more than it is a white movement. It is an anti-capitalist movement, something I like to call small-c communism. Though the great Nick Estes laughed when I said that to him: "Hey! Why not big-C Communism?"

KOLHATKAR: Does young people's increased dissatisfaction with racial capitalism offer hope for an energized abolitionist movement?

GILMORE: Probably.

KOLHATKAR: If you could distill a new post-abolitionist world into just a few words, what would they be?

GILMORE: Well, I've already said "small-c communism." Another way I'd distill the vision would be into a phrase I've been using for more than two decades: Freedom is a place.

3

DYLAN RODRIGUEZ

REJECTING REFORMISM

Dylan Rodriguez is a professor in the Department of Black Study and the Department of Media and Cultural Studies at the University of California, Riverside where he is also the codirector of the UCR Center for Ideas and Society. He was an inaugural 2020 Freedom Scholar and served as president of the Association for American Studies. Alongside Ruth Wilson Gilmore, he is a founding member of Critical Resistance—a California-based grassroots abolitionist organization—and he has been on the frontlines of studying racial injustices and anti-Blackness for decades. His books include *Suspended Apocalypse: White Supremacy, Genocide, and the Filipino Condition* and *White Reconstruction: Domestic Warfare and the Logics of Genocide*.

Throughout his academic career, Rodriguez has infiltrated elite higher education with abolitionist ideals, such as through his 2019 publication in the *Harvard Law Review* of an essay titled "Abolition as Praxis of Human Being." As a veteran activist, Rodriguez has witnessed attacks on the abolition movement alongside surges in interest when policing comes under scrutiny. As a result, he is skeptical of reformist efforts to dilute the demand for dismantling policing and incarceration.

In my August 2021 conversation with him, he articulates the

urgent need to reject reformist tendencies in the movement for police and prison abolition.

❀ ❀ ❀

SONALI KOLHATKAR: You've been advocating for the abolition of prisons for many years. Since the 2020 police murder of George Floyd, we've seen a movement for racial justice that has sparked growing interest in the abolition of prisons and policing. How are the two related?

DYLAN RODRIGUEZ: The link between carceral abolition and police abolition is part of the larger context of asymmetric warfare. I use the term carceral because it's not just about prisons; it's also about jails, detention centers, youth facilities, the incarceration of people who are mentally ill and disabled, and so forth.

In the context of nation-states like the US, I think it is a misnomer to keep referring to these things as exclusively part of a criminal justice and policing apparatus. I think this because what we see in the long archive of transgenerational experiences of people who survive these forms of state violence is that they're giving us accounts that sound more like casualties in a one-sided structure of normalized warfare.

The interesting thing about this is that the state and its supporters tend to use exactly that language, naming it as warfare. This can be seen at local, national, and global levels. For example, they will call forms of state violence a "war on drugs," a "war on gangs," and a "war on terror."

So, I think what we need to understand in terms of an abolitionist analysis is that what we are struggling for is liberation, freedom, protection, and even collective self-defense against these various forms of one-sided warfare.

That's how I draw the comparison. Carceral abolition and police abolition are part of the same continuum of struggle. We cannot have one without the other. We can't talk about police abolition without simultaneously asking: How do we decarcerate people? How do we decriminalize people? How do we get them out of conditions of confinement, detention, and incarceration?

KOLHATKAR: After all, the police are the ones who are feeding people into the system of incarceration.

RODRIGUEZ: That's right.

KOLHATKAR: We know, historically speaking, that there is a direct line between slave patrols and the architecture built to police enslaved people in the past—a line between that and today's modern policing and carceral system. What about the movements to abolish them? Can you draw a line between the movements to abolish slavery and the modern abolition movement which is focused on both police and prisons? And how does today's demand to defund the police fit in?

RODRIGUEZ: There are a couple of lines of connection I'd like to draw here. The first is to recognize the continuity between the historical flow of these forms of anti-Black and colonial state violence and the repression of the various movements for liberation from this violence, particularly from normalized anti-Black policing.

However, the thing we need to keep in mind is that the repression of these movements also has long roots. And I think perhaps the most important thing to return to over and over again is the FBI's Counterintelligence Program (COINTELPRO), especially its operation from the 1950s through the 1970s, which pivoted on the repression of the Communist movement and the US left in general. The program was very focused on the repression and liquidation of Black liberation struggles, especially radical and global revolutionary Black liberation struggles which were drawing connections with international movements against white supremacy and various forms of anti-Blackness and colonialism.

So, I think we have to understand that continuity: how policing has worked, how political repression has worked, and how preemptive political repression has worked. In other words, we have to understand that policing also attempts to neutralize and surveil—in effect terrorize—populations that are prepared to engage in radical freedom struggle in all its forms.

It's critical to indicate that although there are tensions within today's complex spectrum of reformist, proto-abolitionist, and abolitionist movements, all are connected to the long historical archive of Black radicalism that informs, feeds, and empowers these movements.

There's no separability; they're inherently connected. Present-tense forms of abolition are inherently connected to the diasporic Black abolitionist struggle. Part of what the contemporary abolitionist struggle recognizes is the anti-Black chattel relationship—the notion that an entire hemispheric civilization had a relation of deadly ownership over an entire category of beings from the continent of Africa. That fundamental relationship of power has never gone away. It's never been abolished. It's been translated and morphed into various forms of institutional and casual relationships, and it is a structuring aspect of how state power itself works.

Abolitionist struggle recognizes that this foundation of anti-Black chattel has a promiscuous and deadly way of proliferating in such a manner that the same power is replicated through all kinds of institutions, across different historical periods.

It also addresses how anti-Blackness proliferates and periodically targets other populations—people who are not marked as being Black. Folks will say this when they come out of carceral sites and police sites. They'll say, in so many words, and sometimes very explicitly, that the forms of state violence and oppressive power that they experience are things that they understood as being most intimately familiar to Black people.

So, that is a central part of that continuity. I also think understanding this allows us to have a better analysis of the distinctions between reformist and abolitionist agendas, platforms, visions, and struggles. The contradiction that you see arising from some progressive reformist struggles, including elements of the police defunding movement, is that they still have a tendency to replicate the assumption that police power—including forms that are anti-Black—still needs to be part of our everyday lives: Maybe police power just needs to be militantly reformed. Maybe it needs to be controlled. Maybe it needs to be more transparent. Maybe police power even needs to be lessened a bit, right? Sometimes that's what "defunding" means to people.

But there is a stubborn persistence—a stubborn loyalty to policing as a form of power that provides social order, whatever that might mean. One of the primary challenges we face is to begin to foster a way of disaffiliating from this almost religious loyalty to carceral power as that which gives order to the world. That is, I think, a primary part of this struggle.

KOLHATKAR: There was a time when the prison/police abolition movement was seen as fringe and radical, and that seems to have changed in the last few years. Do you feel that, even if there's still a stubborn allegiance to policing, that there is more of a validation of the *idea* of abolition? And if so, is there an analogy to slavery abolition? What I mean is that, for a long time, it was utterly unacceptable to even consider abolishing of slavery, and then suddenly, at some point when there was enough movement behind it, it became acceptable.

RODRIGUEZ: I think there is probably some rough historical continuity between these different moments of abolitionism—call them abolitionist culmination, abolitionist renaissance, abolitionist acceleration—in the sense that we can identify specific historical periods where the concept and the movement seemed to gain broader traction among various communities and constituencies of people.

There are a couple of different sides to what is happening. Number one, I think you're correct that the concept of abolition has accumulated political and cultural traction well beyond what I would've dreamed five, ten, or twenty years ago.

I now experience people trying to affiliate themselves with abolitionist politics and vision in ways I never would've anticipated. So, on the one hand, there's an opportunity there to undertake community-building and movement-building relationships that accompany that kind of traction.

But that comes with a challenge. We live in an age where branding and a certain kind of public-facing identity are oftentimes more important to people than actual, humble participation in the collective struggles that compose these movements.

I also see people who are becoming abolition-curious, which is great. I love it because abolition is an invitation. That's what brought me into this movement. It's like people invite me to be part of it, then we're just feeding off each other, teaching each other, and learning from each other. It's a very humbling but beautiful experience, and it's an invitation.

On the other side of this are people in various professions who are, in a strange sense, opportunistically claiming abolition as a kind of public-facing identity, a new form of self branding and labeling. The problem is that some of these folks are doing this as individuals. They don't have direct accountability or strong affiliation with collectives.

There are also certain bureaucrats and administrative leaders—the planners and architects of state power and sometimes of liberal reformism—who are growing their expertise in expropriating the terms of abolition. They are stealing the terms, deforming them, and repurposing them so that they're feeding into processes and reforms that are counterabolitionist.

I've increasingly seen this in a really disturbing manner. Folks will use abolitionist terms to brand reformist measures that actually reproduce and relegitimize police power, state power, and criminal justice institutions. Some folks have even rebranded reformism as "incremental abolitionism," which is a contradiction in terms.

Incrementalism undermines the collective commitment to think creatively about how we can build forms of infrastructure that create housing security, food security, health security, emotional security, recreational security, and educational security.

That's what security is, right? If you look at the long history of abolitionist movements, that's what people were struggling for. Black diasporic abolitionists and liberationists were struggling to burn down the plantation, to destroy these relations of violent, oppressive power. At the same time, this tradition is all about building community and generating forms of collective security. As with any other movement, there is an element of abolitionist struggle that is in danger of being expropriated by liberal elements. We have to call that out, and that's where the work gets sticky and difficult. We have to call out something when it is not resonating with abolitionist principles of transformation and ends up reproducing state power.

KOLHATKAR: There was a time not too long ago when just saying "Black Lives Matter" was controversial, and then, suddenly in 2020 it was not just acceptable, it was sort of universally embraced, at least in liberal enclaves.

RODRIGUEZ: Yeah. It becomes compulsory.

KOLHATKAR: But then of course, it's not accompanied by action . . .

RODRIGUEZ: That's right.

KOLHATKAR: . . . and it's more performative.

RODRIGUEZ: That's right.

KOLHATKAR: It seems to me that there's this generation of people who are now embracing the idea of it and feeling in their sort of new wokeness that the answers are in front of us and all we have to do is "X, Y, and Z." But folks who've been engaged in the movement for decades are countering it with, "We've already tried X, Y, and Z. And not only do they not work, they end up justifying and validating the same systems that we're trying to break apart." Would that be fair to say?

RODRIGUEZ: Yes, absolutely. What you just marked out in crystallized form is a critical analysis of how reformism is a way of limiting how people think about the outermost horizon of political and cultural change. That's what reformism is, right? It's not quite the same thing as reform.

Reform is about individual tactical measures that may or may not create room for larger efforts toward transformation.

Reformism is a political ideology that borders on a pseudoreligious ideology. It's a notion that the only thing you can do—and the only thing that is acceptable—is to reform an existing system. Such notions serve to police the political and cultural imagination and convince people that there is nothing beyond the horizon of the existing system. That's the problem with reformism.

The other thing you're indicating is that loyalty to reformism involves a devotion to short-term agendas and platforms. It resonates with Saul Alinsky's notion of "Rules for Radicals" from back in the day—the fixation on winnable victories. People want to get wins now. It's a profoundly narcissistic and arrogant way of viewing history.

We need to learn from the long history of revolutionary struggle—Black liberation struggle in particular—that understands that part of being engaged in transformative abolitionist struggle means that you humble yourself to the historical record. The objective is not to see every change happen within the next week or even within your lifetime necessarily, but to exemplify the world you are trying to create while going beyond the limits of pragmatic victories.

Instead of short-term platforms and achievable agendas, people also need to be committed to collective study. There are not nearly enough vibrant, creative, committed forms of collective study happening within movements, collectives, and organizations.

I think this is particularly a problem in the United States, but it is not unique to the United States. I think it's concentrated and exacerbated in the United States because there's such an attachment to immediate political gratification. But I think that when folks are engaged in some form of sustained collective study, that's when we see the most effective forms of revolutionary struggle.

4

NOELLE HANRAHAN

EVOLVING TOWARD ABOLITIONISM

More than thirty years ago, attorney Noelle Hanrahan launched a journalism project called Prison Radio built on a simple idea—give people in prison a platform to tell their own stories.

Hanrahan made a name for herself by producing political prisoner Mumia Abu-Jamal's radio commentaries and helping him publish his first book from prison. In 2001, she told *Stanford Magazine*, "Given the corruption, I am not sure it would even be possible for Abu-Jamal to receive a fair trial now. But I have to believe in the justice system."[24]

After decades of having a front-row seat to injustice, her views evolved toward abolition. Her mentors include Out of Control: Lesbian Committee to Support Women Prisoners, Women Against Imperialism, Dolly Pomerleau of the Quixote Center, Alice Lynd Esq., and the abolition futurism of Joy James.

For Hanrahan, abolition is not an abstract theory. She works with prisoners on death row, in solitary, and those struggling to write and be heard every day. Her teenage son was shot in Philadelphia's Tacony neighborhood. He survived. Hanrahan reached out to the shooter, his family, and the district attorney. She met with them and advocated for the shooter—barely seventeen years old and facing decades in state prison. According to Hanrahan, she told Judge Barbara McDermott that she hoped the incident would be an opportunity for him "to pivot, change, and not have additional trauma imposed by sending him to prison." The impact of the culture of violence and the disposability of poor people, a direct by-product of racial capitalism, has deepened her belief in abolition.

In a wide-ranging conversation, Hanrahan explains why she no longer trusts the justice system and the courts to deliver impartial decisions and how the resources that support those systems need to be reallocated directly to people's needs.

❈ ❈ ❈

SONALI KOLHATKAR: How badly broken is our legal system from the perspective of minimizing harm to individuals and communities? It's supposed to be the place where justice gets decided and meted out, but is it really?

NOELLE HANRAHAN: Simply, it is not broken. Over decades of study and work in the world, I have earned some scars and some knowledge. Juan Gonzales, Mike Davis, Ed Mead, Mumia Abu-Jamal, and Joy James have inspired me to consider how class interests have served by design and adaptation to silence the many and privilege the few. These lenses of critique reveal a system working exactly as planned. Racial capitalism serves the ruling class, the capitalist class, those who want to manage the people who are demanding food, work, bread, and dignity.

For a number of decades now, we have suffered the escalation of tactics by the state against folks who struggle for agency and freedom. Internally, the US sows terror as a method of compelling acquiescence. The system's response to people organizing movements for liberation has been to criminalize, incarcerate, and assassinate.

KOLHATKAR: When discussing abolition, it's sometimes spoken about in terms of ending policing, sometimes in terms of ending prisons, and occasionally in terms of ending the entire criminal justice legal system as we know it. Where do you stand on the issue of abolition?

HANRAHAN: It's been an evolution, but I am firmly an abolition futurist. All the data points to the fact that "American justice"—that special set of relationships, that rubric—is itself criminogenic: It *creates* crime. It is a calculated strategic plan that systematically disenfranchises, imprisons, and divides classes of people. Therefore, we need to divert funding from that apparatus of repression. That includes choking off money to the police and their repressive fraternal organizations. It will require completely transforming the criminal justice system at every level, including the courts.

During the last forty years, mass incarceration has grown immensely. As that was happening, I got my master's degree in criminal justice from Boston University (BU) and my Juris Doctorate law degree from Rutgers because I wanted to understand why the temperature was rising in the boiling pot of water that we are in. At BU, I was studying with a lot of cops and guards who were calling in or zooming in from Bagram Air Force Base in Afghanistan. They were thinking people who wanted to understand what was happening. They also wanted the pay bump that comes with getting a master's. During my law degree at Rutgers, I was studying with those who either wanted to cash in, move up a class notch, or were liberal do-gooders. The frameworks of examination, those allowed in academia, are extremely limited. It amounted to, at best, "tinkering with the machinery of death," not challenging it or asking how to transform the material conditions.

I had to go beyond the classroom to understand what was happening. I had to listen to prisoners.

For instance, the carceral system in the United States is responsible for a national public health crisis. The only way that we are going to get people to have a decent and equitable future is to completely re-envision the entire structure that is killing our people and suffocating our communities. Let's be honest—we all feel it. Whether or not folks can see and identify it as the boot on their neck that's choking them and their children to death, everyone feels it. Paying for people to be warehoused in prisons and for the system of post-incarceration control is preventing us from adequately funding education and health care, and that's driving down our life expectancy.

The violence that's perpetrated by the system on both sides of the wall—the police and the guards—destabilizes our entire culture. The carceral system fuels destabilization, violence, trauma, and disease. Tuberculosis doesn't respect prison walls. Hepatitis C doesn't respect prison walls. Violence doesn't respect prison walls. Guards go home at night, and soldiers come home.

In theory and practice, abolition challenges us to change and interrupt the orderly function of the system. It also challenges us to allow for grace. It challenges me personally to meet the seventeen-year-old shooter of my son Miles and demand that the system pause, not just grind the kid up. Love, not fear, will define the future. As Joy James notes in her unflinching and piercing examination *In Pursuit of Revolutionary Love*, the key to abolition is believing in change, retaining hope, and acting with love.

KOLHATKAR: How does the US compare to other countries in terms of policing and prisons?

HANRAHAN: The United States incarcerates more people per capita than any other country on Earth. That's a fact. Furthermore, the US criminalizes people in a way that's more systemic than most other nations. What other country privileges access to guns the way that the US does? What other country saturates their communities with armed police officers? It's actually surreal. It's not a sane response to crime, health issues, or community issues. So, I think, yes, this country creates crime through policies that are fundamentally unjust, and which seek to commodify and criminalize entire classes of folks in the name of "justice," while promoting the false narrative that they are delivering democracy and security.

The US system of policing and prisons is designed for population control and class war. It criminalizes and penalizes people through fines in vast ways, as was demonstrated in Ferguson, Missouri where much of the population had outstanding fines and could be picked up by police at any time.

KOLHATKAR: Some have said that policing is an extension of the system that was used to control enslaved folks, as well as people after slavery and during Jim Crow segregation. Would you agree that it's basically an extension? We've never truly built the system from the ground up to deliver justice. And therefore, since it was built on injustice, it remains that way.

HANRAHAN: It was designed to normalize inequities, privilege only one sector of the population, and gloss over the essence of liberty with flowery language. It was not designed to liberate or empower all. It was designed to privilege the few—predominantly white men.

I also think it's true that those systems have been evolving. For example, the Thirteenth Amendment doesn't abolish slavery. Instead, it openly normalizes it within the carceral system as "a punishment for crime whereof the party shall have been duly convicted." The US Constitution is littered with racial language that privileges inequities and benefits one class over another.

In Philadelphia, where I live, Larry Krasner, a progressive Democratic district attorney, has said in many venues that everyone knows the reason why we have over-incarceration and such corruption in our police department. It is because police are arresting the most vulnerable populations—people of color and lower-income folks—in part to increase their pay bump for overtime. This has been going on for decades in Philadelphia, where there is a majority-white police force in a majority-Black city. The people who get arrested most are the ones perceived as not having enough power to fight it. Brown and Black people were being sent in an assembly line through the Justice Juanita Kidd Stout Center, and the courts were just approving it.

At one point, I said to Joshu Harris, Philadelphia councilmember Kenyatta Johnson's legislative director, "What's up with this?" He said that everybody knows that's happening because the cops have to pay mortgages on their vacation homes. They have summer homes in New Jersey, or it's their last three years on the force and they want to get that pension bump. To do so, they need to stack up the hours. That's why it's so difficult to fix things. That's the reason we don't have any money or the things that actually foster public safety in Philadelphia.

Another example: I interviewed Barbara McDermott, a sitting homicide judge in Philadelphia, and I asked her why the number of murders being solved was plummeting. She said, "Oh I can tell you why, we told the police they could not chain folks to radiators and beat them into confessing…the police said they knew who was guilty and the courts were not letting them do their job."

Everyone who is living off the system and participating in the system knows that the system of police pay and overtime is completely corrupt. They know that the police have tortured people for decades. These are open secrets in Philadelphia.

KOLHATKAR: Speaking of money, the carceral system—policing, prisons, and the courts—creates a huge resource sinkhole. And the idea of defunding and abolishing police for that very reason was accompanied by a call to start moving resources into the things that would make policing obsolete, such as providing people with all of the things that they need: shelter, food, health care, etc. From an attorney's perspective, what are the legal resources that could benefit from being funded? How could resources be transferred from the courts and put toward things that would make the courts themselves obsolete?

HANRAHAN: Everything that is currently being funded has to be reimagined, justified, or cut. We need social workers, not police officers. We need the community to have health care and jobs. The courts are just there to put a rubber stamp on it. We would have a lot less community destabilization if we could address social inequities and also the problems that have been stoked by defunding our schools, health care, and employment opportunities.

We need that behemoth of a police budget, the billion-dollar police budget in Philadelphia, to be completely reallocated in a way that's going to actually support people's well-being and economic and physical security.

There are other repulsive things that the criminal justice system imposes. It commodifies everything—the mail, phones, even people's bodies. Anybody who is convicted and sent to state prison in Pennsylvania loses their vote. But the rural county where they're incarcerated gets to count those bodies when representation is allocated for national offices and continues to do so even after they're released. Rural counties in Pennsylvania get more congress people because they have three big prisons. That kind of political commodification and stealing of people's agency has to stop.

And yes, abolition is a dream, but we get to dream. We get to dream about a future that doesn't kill our children, and we get to dream about a future that's equitable, where we don't have to watch and witness police brutality on a routine basis. Abolition doesn't exist yet, but it can and will emerge if we work toward it together. As Mumia says, "it takes love, not fear." It takes insurgent imagination. We need to have vision. Thank God for visionaries like Joy James, Abolitionist Law Center, and Law for Black Lives.

As Joy James writes, "If through Revolutionary Love we develop the communal structures, political will, and emotional intelligence to sustain longevity in struggle, then we build capacity to embrace and learn from the survivors of genocide, enslavement, political imprisonment, and mass incarceration. We all need self-respect and self-defense; this democracy is not engineered to meet our needs—hence the organic development of Revolutionary Love addresses our needs."[25]

Lawyers need to show up. The only reason I became a lawyer was because we don't have enough people showing up in court to represent marginalized people. For example, people in prison who had Hep C, which is a curable disease, were dying because they didn't have someone advocating for them. That's one reason why I went to law school. I also went to law school because at Prison Radio we privilege the voices of people on the inside. After decades, it wasn't enough to just broadcast their voices. I also had to bring our correspondents home—to do everything I could to win their release—not just work with them as a colleague.

KOLHATKAR: Earlier we were discussing how the court system really does not validate and foster justice. What could a reimagined legal system look like? Because legal accountability is essential in a functioning democracy, right? I'm thinking of corporate criminals, war criminals, and corruption at the highest levels. If so, what would a functioning democracy's legal system look like?

HANRAHAN: I think having radical and revolutionary accountability, which might be district attorneys who prosecute police and who actually hold people accountable for the crimes they commit against people, is important. I also think we need to elect our own judges.

KOLHATKAR: That happens in some places like in Los Angeles, where I am. Local judges are elected here.

HANRAHAN: Many judges are also elected in Pennsylvania. Mumia Abu-Jamal said that things would've been different for his case if we had started electing judges back in the day. It doesn't take much, but we need to do it. And they need to be people who we vet and trust and who are not going to participate in the assembly line that has become the prison industrial complex.

The current system is like cancer, and it is very capable of adapting. "Reform" is always a nice-sounding word, but it is not what we need. We need radical systemic change. Those in power won't permit reforms that challenge the system, but that's what's needed. We need to challenge the system and transform it, and we have to make the change happen ourselves through organizing, self-care, and mutual aid.

KOLHATKAR: Is the act of electing judges and radical DAs part of the radical reforms needed toward reimagining courts?

HANRAHAN: Demanding what we need is the first step. Accountability is the second. Are those folks going to change?

If not, they need to go. I think we need to vet those people, and we need to make sure that they're really going to do the job that we want them to do. It's difficult to transform this system. I was reading a book this morning about how the Obama administration recognized that the Ferguson issue—the legal issue of making almost all the residents have criminal records—wasn't going to be fixed easily. But it could actually be fixed if the proposals were willing to go far enough.

We need wholesale amnesty. We don't merely need an Innocence Project or a district attorney letting twenty people out of prison. We need all of the arrests that were unjustly done, all of the arrest warrants, all of the people who police incarcerated through incorrect means—that whole class of people—we need all of them to get relief at once. No piecemeal, one person gets released just so we feel better. The system incarcerates whole classes of people. And so, the change we seek needs to be equally weighted. Let me give you an example of what I mean. The promotion of Innocence Projects and public defenders is a necessary stage in propping up a dying criminal justice system by trying to convince the public that justice may come decades later but the system can be fixed. The front-page exonerations are literally used to cover up the problem—to releases some pressure—by pretending that the system works. Public defenders and Innocence Projects are necessary components of keeping the elaborate con going. The con being that we are safer with more policing and prisons.

There was a truth, justice, and reconciliation announcement from Krasner's office in Philadelphia. That's the sort of change that's needed. We cannot move forward without an acknowledgement of the harm—the torture—inflicted on whole neighborhoods. Reconciliation means nothing without truth and justice. The process needs to have real teeth. The perpetrators need to be brought to account. They need to acknowledge what happened, hold people accountable, and free the people who were unjustly convicted—all of them.

KOLHATKAR: It seems as though our criminal justice system is specifically designed to let wealthy folks off the hook because they can hire the fanciest lawyers. Should we reimagine our court system so that an act that arises from someone's financial inability or from their financial distress is not automatically seen as a crime, but rather a result of systemic injustice that requires system change—restitution, rehabilitation, and long-term economic-justice approaches? And then if you are wealthy, you are the one who gets stuck with a public defender who might have a huge caseload because your wealth shouldn't privilege you. Is there a way to turn it upside down so that the rich aren't the ones who are taking advantage of the system that's been sort of rigged for them?

HANRAHAN: The rich are rarely arrested. If we see otherwise, it's usually just an illusion, a mirage. I wish that the DA's budget and the police budget would be reallocated to go after the people that are hurting the community the most. When crime and what's deeply impacting and hurting the most people are analyzed, it's not going to be the people they're currently arresting. It's going to be people who have a much more systemic impact on increasing pollution, gun violence, and crime. There's a lot going on that is not looked at closely enough. The United States is a rich country. Money should not be coming out of the community and flowing to those who are wealthy. That's class war. We need to keep the money in the community, and it needs to increase public well-being, security, education, and opportunity. That's the abolitionist vision.

We know we are succeeding when people have full access to their humanity, when it's not such a hostile environment to breathe in and live in. We know we are succeeding when we no longer have police who criminalize people of color, the poor, protesters, the disabled, and the mentally ill. We need to demilitarize society, and we need to invest all of that money directly into community restoration and reconstruction. That's the abolitionist vision, and it's revolutionary.

KOLHATKAR: How has your work with incarcerated individuals for so many decades influenced you and helped you articulate this vision of abolition? What has made you an abolitionist?

HANRAHAN: We learn from our experiences and grow. My father was arrested when I was nine years old, and my family was dramatically affected by that.

My father had five kids, and it was very hard for my family. It was a benefit in one way because I got to spend a lot of time with my father. He dragged me to every basketball game he refereed and every baseball game he umpired. That was the work he could get. It had a real impact on me.

When I started writing and being a journalist, I was also always looking for a way to hear people. I wanted to listen. When we were covering criminal justice, I just could not cover the story without hearing from the people who were dramatically affected—the people inside and their families. My editors started pushing back and not wanting to hear from the people on death row, for instance, when we were covering the reimposition of the death penalty in California. I knew that was the heart of the story. As a journalist, when you get pushback, you know you are asking the right questions. That has driven me to put a microphone in front of the people who are impacted. It's a different language. It's a different culture. You have to privilege listening. But I've learned an enormous amount from those experiences, and I continue to learn every day from listening to those who are imprisoned.

Much of the abolitionist work that we're seeing now originated inside prison walls and was studied and realized there prior to being motivated on the outside. The organizing I am connected to in Pennsylvania is transformative and led by formerly incarcerated people through the Abolitionist Law Center, the Amistad Law Project, the Coalition to Abolish Death by Incarceration, and the Human Rights Campaign. Also, the groundbreaking example of the work of the Jericho Movement and the Spirit of Mandela to support US political prisoners is illuminating.

Basically, we've got to get people out, and we've got to be the abolitionist reality. We've got to envision it, demand it, and make it happen.

5

REINA SULTAN

8 STEPS TO ABOLITION

Building on the work of veteran activists and academics, a younger cohort of people are pushing abolition-inspired ideas into the mainstream. Reina Sultan is a Lebanese American, Muslim journalist and self-described abolitionist. She infuses her reporting with anti-capitalist ideals grounded in models of liberation that prioritize dismantling policing and prisons and ensuring justice for all, including those with disabilities.

When reformist responses to George Floyd's murder flooded corporate news outlets in 2020, Sultan was among those seeking to steer the discourse away from increased police training and equipment to alternative forms of justice.[26]

She was also part of a small team of people who launched the website "8 to Abolition," in direct response to Campaign Zero's "8 Can't Wait" series of reformist recommendations to fixing policing. The project, which went viral, was an elegant and powerful retort to those who claim that abolition is too complicated, and therefore impossible.

In our February 2023 conversation, Sultan, who is editorial director at The Newsette, shares the backstory to 8 to Abolition and how applying these demands can lead to positive structural change.

SONALI KOLHATKAR: How did the 8 to Abolition plan come about?

REINA SULTAN: Well, the eight-step plan is really a small, condensed understanding of what abolition of policing and the prison industrial complex would look like. It was in direct response to another intervention that was introduced after the murder of George Floyd. There was a reformist agenda introduced called 8 Can't Wait, which was a series of eight reforms that was suggested for cities to implement to reduce police violence by a certain percentage.

Many cities had already done these things. In fact, Minneapolis already had a lot of these in place before George Floyd was killed. I was on X (then Twitter) in the wake of all this, and a friend of mine had posted saying, "Hey, do any abolitionists want to get together and create a response to 8 Can't Wait?"

So, nine other people and I got together and created 8 to Abolition in about twenty-four hours. We worked through the night and came out with this intervention that ended up going viral, which was not anticipated. It seemed like a lot of people wanted a taste of what abolition would look like. They wanted very clear demands that they could make to government officials or express out loud when they were in the streets protesting.

As there are many schools of thought in abolition, 8 To Abolition does not incorporate every single element of what abolition could look like. However, it was easy for us to come together and produce this precisely because there's such a rich amount of abolitionist work being written, and most of that comes from Black women, queer scholars, and other people who have spent a lot of time ideating around abolition. So, we were able to draw from that rich history to put together 8 to Abolition in a short amount of time.

KOLHATKAR: The ideas around abolition of policing and prisons go back decades, at least. There are figures like Angela Davis and her 2003 book *Are Prisons Obsolete?* There's Ruth Wilson Gilmore and many others. It was amazing that in 2020 major media outlets were at least discussing ideas of abolition, even if they didn't necessarily follow through later or take it seriously. Still, they did talk about it, which is pretty big, right?

SULTAN: Yeah, it was wild to see the differences between before and after 8 to Abolition because I had been writing about abolition before George Floyd was murdered. Obviously, he was not the first person to be brutally murdered by police, because policing is brutal and violent. People are killed by police every single day; we just don't hear about it.

This was something that I had been writing about before summer 2020. There were so many people reaching out to me as a journalist, asking me to write about abolition after June 2020. I wish there was still that much vigor and excitement in thinking about ways to break free from what we've considered normal.

KOLHATKAR: Let's talk about what those steps are. The first one might be the most controversial because it has been the most deeply misunderstood, and that's simply "defund police."

"Defund police" is an idea that is not very complicated to explain but it's something that gets turned into a very convenient talking point for the right. How do you explain it in a brief way?

SULTAN: What's great about it is that it's really all in the name. Defund police means defund police. It doesn't mean anything else. There's been a lot of injecting from both the right and from the neoliberal wing of the government that defunding the police means a bunch of other things. But what it means is taking money out of the police budget and diverting it to different things.

Many abolitionist scholars, Mariame Kaba included, call policing and prisons death-making institutions" We want to take money from the death-making institutions and put them into life-giving services, which are things that actually support people rather than create violence.

KOLHATKAR: The second point in 8 to Abolition is "demilitarize communities." Many Americans might respond, "What do you mean by 'demilitarize?' We don't live in a war zone."

SULTAN: I think that if someone says that they don't live in a war zone, they are probably living in an affluent community that hasn't been subjected to the kind of policing that poorer communities are subjected to daily. A lot of people who previously had their eyes closed to this type of thing were able to see it in the media for the first time in 2020.

We see police using military gear when they suppress protests and when they patrol communities. This has been going on for a very, very long time. But I think a lot of people didn't understand how intense this was until they saw tanks in their communities while they protested police violence. We saw this in Ferguson. We saw this in LA after the Rodney King verdict. It's not new, but I think people were not aware of it until recently.

KOLHATKAR: Journalists weren't as aware of it until they witnessed police brutality during the protests in 2020, and they also sometimes became victims.

Let's pivot to removing police from schools, which is step two in the 8 to Abolition plan. Many people, again, don't think about our schools being policed, but they are, especially public schools in low-income communities, right?

SULTAN: Yes, and this is something that has a lot of elements. One of the issues is that we're putting the money that should be going to educating children into policing them instead. It is just a waste of funds. It's not helping kids.

We also now know that the school-to-prison pipeline is a very real phenomenon and that Black and Brown children, as well as disabled children and poor children, are often diverted from schooling into the criminal punishment system. And so, removing police from schools and instead implementing real safety initiatives would better serve children.

KOLHATKAR: School shootings are often the basis for injecting police into schools, but we could just get rid of guns, right?

SULTAN: Right, and I think that especially for that argument it is an unfortunate truth that if you look at whether police are able to stop school shootings, they're actually not. It's not something that is a valid argument because police haven't stopped school shootings. We're clearly not safer with armed police in schools.

KOLHATKAR: The next point in 8 to Abolition is the older idea of freeing people from jails and prisons. There have been long-standing fights in various cities—in places like Los Angeles or Detroit—where people have worked to shut down jails and reduce prison populations, and they're seeing some success even if it's not getting much media coverage, right?

SULTAN: Yes. We want to abolish police, prisons, jails, and other places where people are being held against their will. This is a controversial point for many people. They feel very confused about this. But the point is that putting people in cages is inhumane, and it does not solve any of the problems that it purports to solve.

So, one thing that we can immediately do is decarcerate people from jails where they're being held pretrial. There is no good reason for people to be held when they have not even had a trial yet. And obviously, I'm someone who believes that everyone should be freed from jails and prisons.

This also includes things like clemency for people who are older or disabled. There are so many chronically ill people in prisons and jails who are being brutalized by the pandemic and having a hard time accessing care. It's completely inhumane to keep people in there, especially when governors and presidents have the power to free people immediately.

KOLHATKAR: Let's talk about the criminalization of poverty. That's step five in the 8-step plan: repeal laws that criminalize survival. Please explain this.

SULTAN: This step includes repealing laws that punish people for stealing when they don't have enough money for food. Why should people be punished for their desperation when governments should provide national security by ensuring food and housing for all?

Another thing that is often criminalized is self-defense in situations of domestic abuse and interpersonal violence. When women are being sexually assaulted or raped, they might defend themselves against the abuser and end up in prison. This happens very often. We've seen some pretty high-profile cases of people being held against their will who then kill the person who had been abusing them. And that is just self-defense. There's no reason for people to be locked up for trying to do what it takes to survive. This issue is really widespread, particularly as it relates to women fighting for survival in domestic or sexual abuse scenarios. Survived & Punished is a great organization that highlights that struggle and tries to get people out.

KOLHATKAR: Is this step also related to defunding the police? Because if we funded social services, if we better funded those things that keep us housed and fed and clothed, that's part of removing funding from police, right?

SULTAN: Police budgets are so bloated. They're in the billions. Often police get so much money in overtime. They get new cars all the time. There's all this expensive technology. And there's so much money that we could be spending on people actually getting access to what they need. Instead, we're paying for them to get arrested, beaten up, locked up, and in too many cases killed.

KOLHATKAR: People who support the police unconditionally are often surprised when they find out how much of their own city's budget goes to policing. There are some cities where one-third to half of the entire city budget goes into policing, and everybody else has to fight over the scraps.

Let's keep going. Number six in the 8-step plan is to "invest in community self-governance." What does this mean?

SULTAN: To be very clear, this is not the same as community policing. Community policing is just repackaged policing. Community self-governance is when people who live in a community, not government agencies, are the ones making decisions about their own affairs. They can be tenant unions, street vendors, anything like that. But it's people who are actually being affected by the issues of the community who are deciding what they need to make their community better.

Many kinds of training can be organized to ensure that people know their communities have their back. If there's a problem or an emergency, these trainings teach people to rely on those who live around them and with whom they create these relationships.

KOLHATKAR: Are there examples of this that you can point to?

SULTAN: Yes, I would say that a perfect example could be seen when a huge number of new tenant unions came up at the start of the COVID-19 pandemic. People were out of work, and we weren't quite sure yet if there were going to be relief checks coming, and the eviction standstills weren't going through, or landlords were not abiding by them.

I live in Brooklyn, New York. So, there was the Crown Heights Tenant Union and the Bed-Stuy Tenants' Union who found lawyers, made sure that everybody in the area knew their rights and weren't getting evicted, and helped with rent reductions for people who weren't working. This was an effort by the community, for the community, to ensure that people remained housed.

KOLHATKAR: Step seven in the 8-step plan is to "provide safe housing for everyone." Why is housing so essential? There's a menu of things that everybody needs: food and education, etc., but why specifically focus on housing?

SULTAN: Yes, of course people need food and education and a lot of other things to survive and thrive. But it is extremely difficult to do anything if you do not have safe and secure housing.

Another reason for specifying housing is that people who are unhoused are targeted by the police in a huge way. There are sweeps, people are arrested for using drugs in public or for public urination, and things like that. What are they supposed to do if they don't have a home?

And there's a lot of requirements for people to get housing that are unrealistic. Especially for people who might be struggling with drug addiction or who have certain mental health issues. If we just provided safe housing for everyone, we could cut out so many of the other issues. People would have a lot more opportunity to thrive and feel safe if they weren't having to figure out where they're going to sleep every night.

KOLHATKAR: In many ways, this overlaps with step five, repealing laws that criminalize survival. We see the continued criminalization of the unhoused in cities often run by supposedly liberal mayors, liberal DAs, and so-called liberal police chiefs.

The final step in the 8 to Abolition plan is to "invest in care not cops." I imagine this is very much related to some of the previous steps that we've talked about. Why is this the final step?

SULTAN: I think that it kind of brackets the whole thing. So, if the first part establishes what we are defunding, then this last step outlines what it is that we're funding. So many things that people really need are underfunded in our communities: public transportation, mental health care that is not coercive, etc.

Honestly, a lot of mental health care that is provided to people is almost the same as incarceration because people are held against their will and compelled to do certain things. There are other, non-coercive options that we could be giving people.

We need so many things in our communities. We could have community fridges. We could have more food banks. Public transport could be free. Higher education could be entirely free. We are not funding any of these things because policing and prisons cost so much money. If we weren't putting so much money there, the taxes that we're paying could go towards making people safe and secure in a way that's actually meaningful.

KOLHATKAR: Where has the 8 to Abolition plan gained traction? You mentioned that it went viral in 2020.

SULTAN: I would say that in 2020, the biggest thing that it did was political education. I think a lot of people who had not yet heard of prison abolition or police abolition came to understand what it was all about through this intervention.

We never intended for it to be something that was the end-all, be-all of abolition. We just wanted people to understand that there was another option if we dared to imagine it.

What I did not anticipate—and I don't know if the other cocreators felt this way—but I did not anticipate the turnaround from government officials who had previously said that they were interested in eliminating some part of a police budget and then backed out and became very pro-police.

I think that the politicians we have right now have become very pro-tough-on-crime and back bigger budgets for police. This feels like a direct response to the fact that people actually wanted police to be defunded, actually wanted people to be freed from jails and prisons. This has been such a threat to the status quo that even alleged progressives were like, "No, no, no, no, we're going to make sure that we quell this." And that's what I think we're seeing right now.

People in power are very much trying to ensure that defunding the police never happens. They want to maintain the order that has been in place for decades and stifle our messaging, but abolitionists are still making noise. We're still organizing. We're still pushing for these goals, and we will continue to do so until something changes.

6.

CAT BROOKS

WHAT REALLY KEEPS US SAFEWHAT REALLY KEEPS US SAFE

Cat Brooks is an abolitionist organizer, activist, performer, and host of the radio program *Law and Disorder* on KPFA Pacifica Radio in Berkeley, California. Inspired by her mother, who was an activist for survivors of domestic violence in Las Vegas, Nevada, Brooks has been a fixture in California's political landscape. One of her earliest activist experiences was at Community Coalition in South Los Angeles, which she credits as laying the foundation for her abolitionist work. Brooks later played a central role in the protests against the 2009 Bay Area Rapid Transit (BART) police killing of Oscar Grant in Oakland, California.[27]

Brooks is the cofounder and executive director of the Anti Police-Terror Project (APTP) where she was instrumental in the formation of MH First Oakland, a nonpolice alternative for people experiencing mental health crises.[28] She was also the runner-up in Oakland's 2018 mayoral election, facing incumbent Libby Schaaf.[29] Brooks has worked with impacted communities and families to rapidly respond to police violence and transform policing and incarceration.

When I interviewed Brooks in February 2023, it had been just a few weeks since the brutal police killing of a Black man named Tyre Nichols in Memphis, Tennessee,[30] and days after the

83

sudden killing of a popular local activist, baker, and abolitionist Jen Angel in Oakland during a botched robbery.[31]

* * *

SONALI KOLHATKAR: Tyre Nichols's killing is one of thousands that have taken place every year at the hands of police, and all we hear in response from political leaders are calls for more training, more gear, and more money for police. Are you tired of hearing this?

CAT BROOKS: I've *been* tired of it for a long time. The explosion we saw in Los Angeles after the Rodney King beating in 1992 was a result of the not-guilty verdict given to his assailants—police. The explosion was compounded by all of the rage and trauma people felt because that is what happens and has happened every day in this country since its inception.

The point I've been trying to make in terms of the murder of Tyre Nichols—and we can talk specifically about the police task force involved, the SCORPION Unit[32]—is that there had been at least seven publicized beatings that organizers had raised the alarm about before Tyre was murdered. This is what pretextual stops look like in every city across the nation, every week of every month of every year. This is not an exception to the rule. This is the rule.

KOLHATKAR: One of the other responses to police killings is the desire to hire more police of color, more Black and Brown police. In Tyre Nichols's case, though, there was one white police officer who was fired, and the five that have been charged are all Black. The notion of policing being a white supremacist institution is rarely heard or discussed, right?

BROOKS: Well, first of all, all cops are blue, right? Once you put on that uniform, that badge, you have made a decision to join an institution that, from its inception, has arrested, kidnapped, and killed Black folks and Indigenous folks and Brown folks in the name of profit. That's America's brand of race-based capitalism, and Black folks can also be its agents. White supremacy does not necessarily correspond to the color of your skin. It has to do with what ideological paradigms you are putting forth through your behavior, actions, and choices. Policing in this country is a white-supremacist institution.

KOLHATKAR: What do you make of the fact that President Joe Biden invited Tyre Nichols's parents to his State of the Union address in 2023? This is certainly not the kind of thing we would have seen his predecessor doing. But even though he invited them, he then talked about more police training and reforms. Did Biden pay lip service to justice rather than make an actual commitment?

BROOKS: I have no doubt that he means what he says about wanting more training and diversification. This is the same take we hear over and over again. My question is, when are our leaders, from Biden on down, actually going to look at the data, the logic, and the lived experience of America's most marginalized and admit that the way we do public safety in this country is not working, does not work, and will not work?

How many more gazillions of dollars of our money are we going to allow them to throw away? We are paying to be raped, murdered, incarcerated, beaten, and killed. How many more dollars of our money are we going to lose because they keep doing the same failed thing over and over and over again?

You don't have to agree with me about police or policing. But it's really hard to disagree with the black-and-white facts, data, and numbers.

KOLHATKAR: Whenever there's a discussion of defunding the police or abolishing the police, the counter response tends to be, "How do we live in a world without police, and what about, say, victims of domestic violence who might need to call 911 because they're getting beaten up by their partner or husband?" You have a personal link to this particular question. Tell me about your background and what has given you the insight to identify as an abolitionist.

BROOKS: I'm not only a survivor of domestic violence, I'm also a survivor of state intervention into that violence. One night, when I lived in Las Vegas, my then husband had beaten me pretty severely. He called the police; the police came. Even though I was the one covered in bruises and blood and clearly had been viciously attacked, and even though it was apparent that my husband was fine, I went to jail. And I actually went to jail under laws like mandatory arrest laws and primary aggressor laws that my mother, a domestic violence activist in Nevada, had helped pass in that state.

As a result, I have never called the police again. And what I know now after being in this work for almost two decades is that this is true for Black and Brown women in particular—that we just don't call 911. Wide swaths of the Black and Brown community don't call the police because we know that when we dial that number, it is very rarely help that actually comes. What comes is an institution, or agents of an institution, who are trained to suppress, control, and subjugate, as opposed to help.

And the other thing that folks need to understand is that a world without police doesn't mean a world without accountability. It means that what we're doing right now actually doesn't create safety for anyone. The police have not been defunded.

We've got to talk to our people and help them understand that "defund" and "abolition" mean taking the money that we've been putting into bloated police departments all across this country and redirecting it into the things that actually keep people safe, that actually keep violence from happening in the first place.

Those things are—according to the data and the logic, not just Cat Brooks—housing, mental health support, living-wage jobs, health care, and quality education. Whole, healthy people do not hurt people. Traumatized, wounded, desperate people do.

KOLHATKAR: If we lived in a world where all of these important things were resourced at the time when you experienced domestic violence, how might your trajectory have been different? What would you rather have had at your disposal instead of the police?

BROOKS: Well, I would have liked to have what we've been able to create here in Oakland and Sacramento, Mental Health First, where you can dial a non-911 number. You get a caring, trained volunteer on the other end of the line who's going to help you create a participant-determined pathway to your health and safety.

If dispatch is necessary, it's not a badge and a gun that comes. It's counselors, EMTs, or nurses who can address medical concerns that may be present.

We also need funding for safe houses. When I was a victim of domestic violence, I needed to leave, but where was I going to go? For situations like that, we need safe houses.

And we need counseling that addresses the whole family— both the cause of the harm and its consequences —particularly when children are involved. And that's what I would have wanted to walk into instead of the nightmare that was a DA determined to prosecute and months of fear and terror that actually empowered the perpetrator to harm me more.

KOLHATKAR: You were the victim in that case, and you were the one who was arrested?

BROOKS: I was arrested, and the DA, who I remember very clearly as this red-faced, angry man, seemed to get joy out of the fact that he was going to prosecute me.

I want to let folks know I was eighteen when I was going through this. So, you can imagine how terrified I was. It feels weird to say I was lucky, but my abuser was trying to get me to come home. As a result, he actually told the truth on the stand, and my case got dismissed. But far too often that's absolutely not how things go. There are thousands of women who are locked behind bars because the state responded in the wrong way to them being abused.

KOLHATKAR: It sounds like victims and survivors of domestic violence in our current system get revictimized or become retargeted by either the same or even a different kind of violence, layer upon layer of it, and basically risk further harm instead of being able to have access to resources that reduce harm. But solving it is not rocket science. What you are saying sounds like a very reasonable thing, and yet in city after city we're seeing money being taken away from the types of resources that survivors of domestic violence need and instead being put toward policing. How are we allowing this?

BROOKS: We have had more than fifty years of conducting the failed experiment of giving too much money to law enforcement. Most of America has been lulled into accepting this idea of giving a lot of money to police. The idea is backed up by what we call copaganda. It's backed up by setting budgets. It's backed up by the BS that police associations put out—that "police keep us safe." Most of us can't even imagine a world without law enforcement, and the amount of energy and effort it takes for an organizer to have one by one conversations is huge. But those, along with the creation of models that can be replicated, are going to be what it takes to change things.

I am heartened, though, that these conversations are happening. Because the other thing that Biden said that I am almost bowled over by—not that I give him props for very much very often—is that when cops are responding to domestic violence, they need a psychologist.

I think we are seeing a sea change and, if we're smart as organizers, we can exploit this point in time to create a watershed moment where folks understand that badges and guns are not what we need to respond to community crises. Trained, caring, and compassionate community members are what we need instead.

KOLHATKAR: What are some of the ways in which you can counteract the habit of calling 911 in an emergency? If someone breaks into your home, and you're terrified of calling the cops, what other options are there?

BROOKS: When people talk about abolition, they usually think about tearing down laws and norms. But abolition is about building, right? It is about building equitable, just, and humane systems that will work for everyone.

This is one of the fights I used to have with folks here in Oakland when they would say, "Never call the police, ever," and I'd say, "Well who's going to come then?" So, when my seventy-year-old neighbor sees someone being gunned down in front of her house in broad daylight, are *you* coming? Because if you're not coming, then you should hush—and those are often people that don't look like me and that also took myself and my organization to task.

We are responsible for creating the world that we want. Organizing is what gets the goods. We are responsible for creating these replicable models, and we need to stop begging the state for the money, the resources, etc., to create these models.

Mutual aid is a pathway to creating models that produce results people can see. What we've seen here in Oakland is that once the Mental Health First program was available and folks saw it could actually work, it then became their preference. We need to replicate that in as many cities as possible. And yes, it's a long, slow climb, but that's the only way that we are going to get there.

The other thing I want to say is that we have to be really focused on communications. We've got to be talking to people, and not just the people who agree with us. We have to figure out how to talk to folks who aren't exposed to left-wing politics. How do we talk to them? How do we use data, logic, and lived experience to appeal to people's common sense along with their heartstrings?

KOLHATKAR: Tell me what you've achieved in Oakland through your work with the Anti Police-Terror Project and how you envision that work moving forward?

BROOKS: We're taking one issue-area at a time. People have been talking about "divest-invest" for a long time, but with respect to "Defund the Police," we gave birth to that terminology right here in Oakland eight years ago. And it means taking money away from law enforcement and investing it in things that are actually going to keep communities safe. We were laughed out of rooms for a really long time, even by folks who we considered on our side.

But now, what we've managed to do is create a "Reimagining Public Safety" process here that will need to be addressed in the next budget cycle, despite attempts by the prior mayoral administration and some of the folks on city council against it. We've impacted the public debate. We've built deep relationships with the community. We've launched Mental Health First, both here and in Sacramento. We remain the only non-911 response to mental health crises in the area.

We partnered with labor and organizations that work with formerly incarcerated folks. We pushed for there to be a community advisory board, for those impacted to be able to get living wage jobs, and for there to be communication between the city and the grassroots organizers.

Primarily, we were responding to mental health crises. We just released our guide for intimate partner violence after three years of work, and we're going to build a local model to respond to intimate partner violence without the carceral state. After that, we plan to tackle substance abuse.

We've been doing this all while fighting the city council for a budget that invests in things like violence interrupters. That's not the work that *we* do, but we've got comrades on the ground from the neighborhoods where violence is happening who we work with every day. Those are the folks who can stop the violence before it occurs in the first place.

We're never going to stop beating the drum. Many people who rang the alarm bell about the economic pandemic that came on the heels of the COVID-19 pandemic were ignored. If we want it to stop, we've got to address *everyone's* basic needs.

KOLHATKAR: In February 2023 your community lost an activist who was also a baker, Oakland's most popular baker, Jen Angel, who ran Angel Cakes Bakery. She was a friend of mine as well, and she was a victim of a horrific, violent robbery. The message that her community and close-knit family and friends put out was that if there was an arrest made in her case, the city should pursue restorative justice and all available alternatives to traditional prosecutions because those were her values. I'm wondering what your thoughts are on that.

BROOKS: First of all, deep condolences to all who had personal relationships with Jen Angel. I'm very close to a lot of folks who were part of her immediate community. This is a great loss for Oakland and beyond.

We have a new district attorney in office who is looking at what the alternatives could be to the carceral state. It is shameful to see some of the nasty, vile things that people are saying in response to what Jen's family is asking for.

I've been trying to be careful and not speak out of turn. I will just say that whoever committed these horrific acts more than likely comes from a background where they didn't have the resources necessary to build successful, thriving lives. They are probably coming from a background that was full of violence and trauma and pain. Throwing them into one of the most violent institutions known to man, and then spitting them back out in a few years—because they will come home—with no resources or support is exactly how we perpetuate violence in our communities.

KOLHATKAR: And it wouldn't bring Jen back . . .

BROOKS: It would never bring Jen back. And that is the biggest point that abolitionists often make, right? That's how I became an abolitionist, when I was thinking about my own sexual assault, which had prevented me from saying I was an abolitionist for so long, until I realized that the healing I was looking for had nothing to do with the person who harmed me sitting in a cage. I wish that he had been a whole enough person to not have harmed me in the first place. So how do we do that?

7

EUNISSES HERNANDEZ

DEFUNDING THE POLICE

Abolishing police, courts, and prisons requires power, especially the power to hold the purse strings. Choosing what our tax dollars do and do not fund is one way abolitionists translate vision into reality.

In 2022, a young Latina abolitionist moved from the world of community organizing into the world of politics to do just that. Eunisses Hernandez is the daughter of Mexican immigrants to Southern California. She came of age in an era of broken promises that can be traced back to the reforms emerging from the 1992 Los Angeles uprising.

As a cofounder of the Los Angeles–based organization La Defensa, Hernandez was instrumental in mobilizing opposition to jail expansion and crafting local legislation to divert money away from policing and into community resources. She and her fellow organizers dubbed their agenda "Care First, Jails Last."

Few activists who identify as abolitionists have the opportunity to put their politics into practice, especially those as young as Hernandez. In an interview conducted just weeks before she won her election to the Los Angeles City Council in 2022, Hernandez articulated how abolitionist principles would continue to shape her work.

***

SONALI KOLHATKAR: Why are you running for the Los Angeles City Council?

EUNISSES HERNANDEZ: I'm running for office because I live in a district that has had the same representation for the last nine years, and there's been a vacuum in leadership. For the last nine years, we haven't seen any ordinances to address keeping people housed. We see that Chinatown has no hospital. We've seen a ten percent decline in the Latino community in my neighborhood. That's not been by accident, but intentional, through evictions and increases in rent. And the person who's been representing us, Gil Cedillo, has a lot of power in keeping people housed because he is the chair of the Housing and Homelessness Committee.

I've recognized that there's a serious urgency in my community. Many people won't last another four years because they'll be impacted by gentrification and evicted. So, I stepped up, and I didn't have to.

The work that I'm doing in my day job with La Defensa is transformational. We have four people, women, who are running for judgeship in LA County. Nowhere else in California is there a slate of judges like this or a place where we're having actual success in building out alternatives to incarceration and passing ballot measures to move money out of the carceral system.

We've been successful with that here in LA County. But it feels like LA City is still going backwards, still going towards the commodification of housing and people. I want to bring a "Care First" vision of caring for our communities down to City Hall.

KOLHATKAR: Let's go back to the Los Angeles uprising of 1992. It was such a big turning point for the city, and it was a shocking chapter in the nation's history. Can you tell me a little bit about what that set of events means to you? Is it something that you have thought about?

HERNANDEZ: I was born in 1990, so I was two when the uprising happened. I'm 32 right now. When I think about how those moments have influenced our work today, it's a constant reminder that not many things have changed, that we have taken some steps towards progress, but the powerful systems that have harmed us—law enforcement, special interest groups, and corporations—have continuously beat all the efforts that we've made because we're not in a better place in regard to police and community relationships.

In fact, we have one of the largest prison populations in the country and even the world. There are thousands of people in our LA County jail system—over 6,000 of them—simply because they can't pay their bail to get out.

And so, when I think about those moments, I think about how we have grown in certain areas, like around solidarity between Black, Brown, Indigenous and other people of color, low-income communities, and others. And so that's what's given us the power to be successful in stopping a $3.5 billion jail plan here in LA County.

But the riots and violence that happened remind me that we have to push for change constantly. We have to ensure we are not leaving anybody behind, not giving more money and power to systems that harm us, and not building things that we'll have to destroy in the future.

There is a jail in my district that has sat empty for decades. It represents a history of terrible harm and violence. I want to see it reimagined into something that builds up our community: a hub for resources and services that helps correct for the harms of the past. We have a huge need for housing, for green space, for community centers. And yet, we have this vacant building sitting there slowly degrading. It's not something that we take lightly; we are always talking about it and reminding ourselves what we're up against.

KOLHATKAR: One hallmark of the 1992 uprising was that communities of color were pitted against one another. There were very serious tensions. In the end, more than sixty people— mostly people of color—were killed in the uprising. City authorities and the federal government claimed to try to figure out what was wrong, but it was mostly just lip service. There were so many commissions, investigations, and studies. There were initiatives such as Rebuild LA. Have you seen any positive outcomes from any of those efforts?

HERNANDEZ: When you ask me that question, I think about people like Andres Guardado, the eighteen-year-old Latino security guard who was shot and killed by police while on patrol[33]. I think about Destiny Ortega who died in the women's jail. I think about all the lives we've lost to police violence: people shot up by the Sheriff's Department who ended up in jail and in the hospital. If things had actually changed after Rodney King, we wouldn't be seeing continuous loss of life at the hands of police.

I still don't see the level of investment that needs to be made in our communities, like direct investment in social safety nets that keep people housed and employed. Right now, many people I know owe thousands of dollars in rent. We are in a mess *because* of state-sanctioned police violence, and nothing has been done to change their internal systems.

Policing in the United States originated when white enslavers created patrols to catch Black people who had escaped to freedom. American law enforcement is clearly rooted in racism. I don't see much change since the Rodney King uprisings in US systems. I think there are simply more video recordings of these incidents happening, and many people are just numb to it now.

KOLHATKAR: It seems as though city officials did not see what happened in the uprising as a direct outcome of social factors like unemployment and poverty. Obviously, the riots were directly triggered by people seeing the injustice of Rodney King's assailants being acquitted. But the looting, the burning down, much of that was the result—would you agree?—of long-simmering anger in the community. Instead of funding services, the city just kept putting police on the streets, and instead of treating poverty and unemployment as social ills, the city treated them as problems of policing.

HERNANDEZ: Yes, yes. Even in the mayoral debates, people were asking for more law enforcement and more police because they thought that was the solution, but it was not. Paying more people to have guns and badges in our communities doesn't make us safe.

The safest communities are those with the most resources, such as the Los Angeles Westside. When you think about celebrities who are going through crises, they have seemingly endless access to services. But here in our communities, when someone is having a mental health crisis in front of their house most of the time the only option that we have is to call 911.

When law enforcement shows up, they often hurt or kill people. I've worked with families who have called 911 for help when their loved one is having a mental health crisis. Within eight seconds of law enforcement showing up, their loved one is dead. We have not invested in the things that will help our communities thrive. I don't think that the people in charge have learned a thing.

For so long, the power in places like City Hall has been dictated by the special interest groups, entities, and people who have the money to influence politicians and establish systems that work for them. But those systems only work for them, and not for workers, people of color, and the communities who have been targeted, incarcerated, and killed by those same systems at disproportionate rates.

Politicians rarely talk about how bodies are commodified by incarceration, particularly the bodies of Black, Brown, and Indigenous people. Bureaucrats never talk about the racial injustice that pervades US systems. They create departments to try to address anti-Blackness and racism in their bureaucracies, but you have to look at the policies, their implementation, and where the money goes.

Most of the money that we have in LA City—more than $3 billion of our locally generated tax dollars—goes to incarcerate and criminalize people, not to educate, employ, and house them.

KOLHATKAR: If you had a magic wand that you could wave to redirect some of that $3 billion into the right places, where would you choose for it to go? And if you become a member of the city council, you could have some of that power—at least one vote out of several—right?

HERNANDEZ: Yes. That's a great question.

The answer is participatory budgeting. I love it, and we need more of it. If I had a magic wand, I would invest in creating access to services in every part of the city, particularly mental health services and a spectrum of drug treatments, not just Twelve Steps or Alcoholics Anonymous.

Maybe some people need Medicaid-assisted treatment. Maybe some people need access to other harm-reduction programs such as clean-needle exchange programs. The point is to have life-affirming responses in place when these crises occur.

The second piece is to keep people housed. We need to do whatever we can to make sure that people are not evicted from their homes because they can't pay rent or because of other policies that are racially unjust or based on gender discrimination.

Women are one of the biggest groups of people experiencing homelessness right now because of high levels of intimate partner violence and low access to stable housing. Young LGBTQ+ people who are transitional age comprise another big chunk of the population who are experiencing homelessness. And whether they're LGBTQ+ or not, many of them fall through the cracks when they've aged out of foster care but aren't eligible for other services.

I really want to increase services, jobs, and housing to protect these youth, particularly undocumented youth. In MacArthur Park, which is in my district, and in many other parts of the city, we're seeing undocumented youth who don't qualify for the Deferred Action for Childhood Arrivals (DACA) program. This drives them to desperation and increases their vulnerability to gangs.

We clearly need to create opportunities for these young people to be able to make money through different programs and jobs that the city can develop.

I keep going back to the question "what is a safe community?" A safe community is where people have stable housing, support, thriving wage jobs, health insurance, free public transportation that's accessible everywhere, and clean air and water.

Right now, we have more than 700 oil wells in my district. We need to be closing them down and turning them into green spaces because more than seventy percent of the people in my district live in apartments, and many of them don't have green spaces.

So, what I imagine the best community being is not pie in the sky. It's not like this community doesn't exist. It *does* exist, and it exists in other parts of this county that have more resources. But even when there's a lot of resources, you need to have people who are willing to make decisions by prioritizing people and community, not private profit and commodification.

We could do a lot, such as invest in our youth and elders. These are not dreams. These are real, and we're going to make them happen.

KOLHATKAR: What are some grassroots efforts that have been successful and could potentially be used as models for moving forward?

HERNANDEZ: I can give two examples. One is in LA County, where we—others who are part of a coalition called Justice LA and I—stopped a $3.5 billion plan to build a new women's jail in Lancaster and a new jail for people with mental health needs in downtown LA.

We convinced them to stop it by bringing psychiatrists, union workers, and doctors who work in the ERs and the jails to testify that moving forward with the mental-health jail facility was not going to make people well or keep us safe.

Once we convinced them to cancel those contracts, we worked with the county to develop what's called "the Care First, Jails Last report." This report has 114 recommendations that we cowrote with various county departments to create a pathway for our communities to access care without criminalization and prevent the carceral system from accessing our communities.

For example, a 988 access phone line that already exists at the federal and county level is now being implemented at the county level because we pushed for it. It's an alternative to 911 so that people can call and get a mental health, crisis-response team. They exist, and we need more in LA County.

Many of the recommendations in "the Care First, Jails Last report" were adopted by the Board of Supervisors. We created a department within LA County called the Alternatives to Incarceration initiative where they're actually implementing the report's recommendations. One of the initiative's main goals is to get the more than 6,000 people who are in our LA County jail system awaiting trial released. A key feature of the initiative is a community-based, non-carceral pretrial service, such as text reminders to get people back to court.

That's just one example of how we stopped the contract to build new jails and developed a plan for what could be done instead.

That plan is actually being implemented with money from the county that we looked for. The county isn't going to look for money on its own.

We also worked on Measure J, a ballot initiative that I cowrote with colleagues, which was passed by LA County Voters in November 2020. The goal of Measure J is to move ten percent of locally generated tax dollars into two buckets. The first is community investment, such as youth services, minority-owned businesses, and housing. The second bucket is alternatives to incarceration—committee-based, non-carceral pretrial services, mental health services, drug treatment, and access to jobs.

Two million voters in LA County said, "yes, we want to move our money to these things." In year one—which was last year—we wrote a report with recommendations called "the Measure J Year One Spending Plan." The report calls for $1.5 million to be invested in youth hubs, and $52 million to be invested in access to mental health and drug treatments.

And so, this report outlines essentially what we talked about: if you had a hundred million dollars, what would you do with it? This is what we did with it. We moved the funds through a ballot initiative and determined where that money went. We were able to uplift the communities that needed the money the most, which were Black transgender women, elders, young people, and other people from the LGBTQ+ community. It was a phenomenal opportunity for us to build off of all the budget advocacy work we had done to get it approved and implemented.

Measure J Year One money is already beginning to be dispersed into community resources, and we're talking about year two, another hundred million dollars in Measure J money.

The last example I'll give involves the LA County Gender Responsive Advisory Committee, which I chaired. This committee was created in response to plans for building a gender-responsive jail for women. We shifted that whole body to say, "look, we're now going to focus on trying to figure out the ways we can end the incarceration of Two-Spirit, transgender, gender diverse, LGBTQ+, and cisgender women in LA County and build out the services we need to care for them in community."

I know that was a long answer, but we have had a lot of success in moving funds out of the carceral system and into community, from jail construction to housing and care.

And that's why I'm also running for city council: because we built the coalitions, the groups of people who have been politically educated and engaged on these issues, to support us moving forward into the next level of our advocacy and moving forward policies and budgets that actually meet the needs of our communities.

I'm running against Gil Cedillo, a career politician who's been taking dirty money—over half a million dollars—from special interest groups, law enforcement groups, and developers. We've gotten thousands of dollars in contributions from developers, and we've returned it because we are committed and accountable to community.

Eunisses Hernandez went on to win her seat on the LA City Council weeks after this interview was conducted.

8.

IVETTE ALÉ-FERLITO

JUDGING THE JUDGES

Most abolitionists agree on the need to dismantle systems of policing and prisons. Few tackle the courts. But the judiciary is central to the carceral system, performing that crucial middle step between arrest and imprisonment. Many who study courts find them to be dehumanizing spaces that airbrush a veneer of legitimacy on mass incarceration.

La Defensa, a Los Angeles–based grassroots organization, is one of a growing number of groups shining a light on the conduct of local judges as part of the project of abolishing the judiciary. Ivette Alé-Ferlito, La Defensa's cofounder and executive director, is a formerly undocumented queer femme who has been organizing and leading anti-carceral campaigns in California for nearly a decade.

Alé-Ferlito has helped found and lead multiple coalitions, including JusticeLA and ReimagineLA, supporting historic victories including ending LA County's $3.5 billion jail expansion plan in 2019.

In two interviews conducted in March and June 2023, Alé-Ferlito articulated the deep harm perpetrated by courts and explored the tools that La Defensa has created to hold judges accountable while working to curtail their power and ultimately abolish the system.

＊＊＊

SONALI KOLHATKAR: If people are considered innocent until proven guilty, why are so many people jailed?

IVETTE ALÉ-FERLITO: That is a great question. A huge swath of the people incarcerated in our jails haven't been convicted yet. There are two primary mechanisms by which people are detained. One is the use of money bail. When a person is arrested, a judge might offer that person a bail amount as a way of buying their freedom until their trial. As a result, those who have wealth are able to buy their freedom through the process of bail, and those who don't have wealth remain incarcerated for weeks, months, or even years until they have their day in court. The process of buying freedom through money is therefore an inherently racist and classist system.

Those who have wealth, especially generational wealth, are often folks with privilege, white folks.

But when we talk about those most impacted by incarceration—predominantly communities of color, immigrant communities, and folks without wealth—they remain incarcerated and can lose their jobs, lose custody of their children, and lose their homes. So, the ramifications of being jailed when you are legally innocent are vast.

But there's a second mechanism that keeps people jailed: preventative detention. A judge has the option to say, "You know what, I'm going to detain this person. I'm not going to set bail for them." We saw this become popular at the federal level in the 1980s with the Bail Reform Act of 1984, which really propelled the use of preventative detention.

At the federal level, although there isn't a system of money bail, the judge can decide to detain a person. From the judge's perspective, they don't want the person being re-arrested for something, and then the judge's name and face is splashed on the front of the *New York Times* or the *LA Times* as being responsible for letting them out.

In fact, the vast majority of people who are allowed to defend themselves from a position of freedom are actually able to successfully fight their cases. The fear that judges have—and the power that they have to detain people without a conviction—has propelled an increase in jail populations throughout the United States.

KOLHATKAR: There has been a bail reform movement to address these issues, no? In California in particular, the Humphrey decision establishes that detaining a person prior to their trial solely because they cannot afford bail violates their rights. Why wasn't this enough?

ALÉ-FERLITO: The basis of *Humphrey* is that courts and judges must consider someone's ability to pay when setting bail amounts. So for example, if someone is unemployed, if they are houseless, their ability to pay may very well be zero. And what we've seen in practice here in LA County—and I assume this is also happening across the state and across the country—is that judges will sometimes set a bail amount of a dollar. Sometimes, however, even one dollar is too much for someone who is unemployed and houseless. We've seen instances where the public defender that's assigned to their case will attempt to pay that dollar.

That is so indicative of the way the carceral system works. Even though *Humphrey* says that bail must be set at affordable rates, judges are not applying the law. In fact, they are practicing illegal acts in the courtroom by not applying *Humphrey*. The Civil Rights Corps has sued LA County and the LA Superior Court for not implementing *Humphrey*. We can see laws being passed, but by and large judges are unaccountable. There are very few mechanisms to hold judges accountable.

Yes, judges can be elected, but most people don't know that or are not well informed about judicial elections or who these candidates are. So, one of the very few mechanisms of accountability that we have—elections—are insufficient at the moment because people don't know about them and are not adequately informed about what happens in the courtroom. As a result, judges can often act independently.

KOLHATKAR: Judicial candidates are oftentimes the part of one's ballot that people tend to leave blank, or they scramble at the last minute to try to dig around online to see if they can find any information because judges don't get that much media attention. Tell me about the tool that your organization, La Defensa, created to give voters accurate information on judges.

ALÉ-FERLITO: It's called Rate My Judge, and it's like Yelp for judges. We rely on community reviews from folks who go into the courtroom, who either have their day in court or who are a family member of someone who is going inside. Public defenders, court interpreters, and whoever's in the courtroom are all able to go on our website and leave a review for a judge based on everything from how well they follow the law, to their decorum, to whether they were fair. These reviews help paint a picture of a judge's behavior in the courtroom.

We're expanding the site with our upcoming Court Watch program to integrate additional data around the implementation of the *Humphrey* decision, for example, to make sure that we provide voters and the community with a full picture on judicial behavior. This full picture helps inform which judges folks want to vote for.

If a judge goes to Harvard or some other prestigious school, that doesn't give me information about how they're treating my community. The vast majority of judges are former district attorneys—former prosecutors who come from a prosecutorial background and have a lens of conviction. This is really a motivator for prosecutors: how many folks can they convict? That's the culture of the bench. It comes from a background of law enforcement.

But when we're able to diversify the bench—when we're able to make judicial races competitive with more women, more people of color, and more folks from a public defense background—then we'll be able to shift the approach of the bench and how they're treating our community members, in addition to exposing them through our Rate My Judge tool.

Our Rate My Judge site is completely anonymous for individuals, especially if they're in ongoing cases. In order to protect their anonymity, all of our reviewers are anonymous, but the reviews reflect folks who engage with the courts. We have eyes and ears through all vehicles and all community members that are in the courtroom.

KOLHATKAR: Let's talk about how the judiciary is diversifying. Holly Hancock, who started out as a public defender and was elected to LA County Superior Court, is a rare example of a public defender becoming a judge. Tell me about Hancock and why she's so significant.

ALÉ-FERLITO: Holly Hancock was part of the Defenders of Justice slate that we backed. In 2022, La Defensa launched a Political Action Committee (PAC). We knew we didn't just want to expose judges; we wanted to help transform the judiciary and insert folks on the bench who have experience in public defense and civil rights.

We created the Transforming the Judiciary Coalition with other partners to help identify who could be a good candidate, asking the questions of who would be willing to take the risk, who has alignment in values and could support diversions and alternatives to incarceration rather than just leaning into a prosecutorial approach to the bench.

Through that process we identified four candidates: the Defenders of Justice, four amazing women who were either civil rights attorneys or public defenders. Holly Hancock, who has a deep history of support from the community, was one of the candidates. She had run before in a previous cycle, but lost. What we wanted to do in the 2022 cycle was create support so that those who are running for the bench don't have to do it alone and know that the community is behind them. Holly Hancock, having run before and with her experience as a successful public defender defending our community members, really rose to the top and won her election.

We're incredibly proud of her. She is the first Black woman public defender to ever be elected to the LA County Superior Court, which is historic.

KOLHATKAR: Do you see this work in holding judges accountable via reviews and transforming the judiciary as part of an abolitionist approach to criminal justice?

ALÉ-FERLITO: That's a great question. Abolition is not just about abolishing brick-and-mortar jails and prisons. Abolition is not just dedicated to ending law enforcement and cops. Law enforcement takes many forms. It takes the form of probation officers who surveil our communities. It takes the form of district attorneys who prosecute members of our communities. And it takes the form of judges who ultimately convict and incarcerate our community members.

Judicial accountability is part of our steps toward abolition because we're exposing the behavior of judges. We expose judges as some of the most unaccountable actors within the prison industrial complex, actors who don't get a lot of attention.

Because they act as a separate branch of government, judges have the ability to incarcerate our folks with impunity. In cases of pretrial incarceration, for example, they are not even following the law. Exposing that is step one.

We also want to do harm reduction, and that means replacing judges and winning seats that would otherwise be held by former prosecutors. We want to increase diversity, but not just diversity in terms of gender and race diversity. We want to include diversity of legal backgrounds because that helps shift the culture. It is more of an indicator of alignment with our values.

For example, if we have a Latina woman who's a former prosecutor, she may represent more racial diversity on the bench, but that doesn't necessarily shift the needle in terms of how often our community members are prosecuted and convicted.

In order to have real transformation, we need to have diversity of thought and diversity of legal backgrounds. It's a harm-reduction measure.

Ultimately, the judiciary is not the right vehicle for accountability. We cannot depend on a single person to decide whether our community members should be incarcerated when they haven't been convicted. It is incredibly significant that we have given up our power to judges for so long. And now we're taking steps to take back that power.

Legal action is also part of the road to stripping the judiciary of power, like we're seeing with Civil Rights Corps, an organization dedicated to challenging the legal system and forcing the courts to apply *Humphrey*. It's a policy change to strip the judiciary of power. All of that is working towards abolition— stripping the system of power and diverting resources to vehicles of community-based accountability that actually take people's needs and strengths into consideration. This serves to address the root causes of harm rather than just putting a Band-Aid on the problem and shutting someone in a jail cell.

KOLHATKAR: How can your work in Los Angeles be replicated elsewhere?

ALÉ-FERLITO: I'm glad you asked that because we are part of a national movement. What we're seeing in places like New York is community members actually exposing data about judicial behavior. For example, there is a nonprofit organization called Scrutinize in New York which is creating a ratings system for judges. It uses data on judicial behavior to rate how carceral a judge is.

We're seeing progressive abolitionist folks run for judicial office. We saw Franklin Bynum in Texas run for office and win. Progressive women in Nevada and in the Bay Area of California are running for office and winning. More progressive folks and abolitionist folks are throwing their hat into the ring for judicial office and are winning.

Community members are exposing judicial behavior and creating alternatives. Groups like Silicon Valley De-Bug in California are creating a system of participatory defense to support community members when they have their day in court.

The Bail Project helps people get released and then connects them to services, which we know are actually more effective than incarceration. Providing services and support so folks can return to court is vastly more effective in the long run and better for the health and wellness of the individual and their families and communities.

KOLHATKAR: Rather than being appointed, if judges across the country were elected and held accountable with tools like Rate My Judge the way that judges in LA County are, would that be enough to hold judges accountable? Why isn't it enough to simply reform the judiciary and shine a light on it so that it does what it's supposed to do?

ALÉ-FERLITO: The judiciary does what it was designed to do—extract poor people, Black people, immigrant people, people with mental health needs, and other people who are not considered part of what white supremacy would like to include in society. In this sense, the judiciary is functioning the way it's supposed to.

What we're trying to do with Rate My Judge and with empowering voters to make more informed decisions is a form of harm reduction. It's a first step in informing our community members that they have power and leverage over judges. Rate My Judge also exposes how judges' behavior contributes to incarceration and other systems of harm in our communities.

The next step is to disempower the judiciary altogether. This can be achieved through state and local policy measures. For example, if we pass legislation that limits the circumstances in which a judge can hold someone in jail without a conviction, that will help reduce the power of the judiciary.

We want to expose them and contract their power simultaneously.

KOLHATKAR: In your mind, is there *anything* of value that a judiciary could perform to hold the powerful accountable? I'm thinking of white-collar criminals, corporate criminals, and politicians who abuse their power. Yes, the judiciary was not really designed to hold the powerful accountable, but can it be redesigned to do that?

ALÉ-FERLITO: Part of the beauty of abolition is creating the space to reimagine what accountability looks like. What you're referencing is so important: being able to use the law to protect people against power, to protect the vulnerable against corporations and institutions. That's what our system should be doing. But it was fundamentally not designed to do that.

And so, part of reimagining justice involves thinking about

how we can create systems of accountability that are independent from the structures that were designed to oppress us.

I think the idea of maintaining a power structure and then telling that power structure to have a different mission would be a very difficult undertaking.

Constructing something that we don't have to dismantle in the future is a fundamental principle of abolition. Our mission as abolitionists is to construct something from the ground up that is independent from our current judicial systems and rooted in community, rooted in justice, and rooted in protecting people.

KOLHATKAR: So, being proactive rather than reactive, creating regulations that protect us from businesses and protect us from politicians?

ALÉ-FERLITO: Yes.

KOLHATKAR: Let's focus on resources. The slogan "Defund the Police" is one that many people are familiar with and is based on the idea that police suck up too many resources from our city budgets while the programs that actually keep us safe are always starved for resources. Can the same be said about the judiciary?

ALÉ-FERLITO: Absolutely. The budgets for the judiciary have been climbing for the last twenty years, and the increases in judicial spending are reflected in the expansion of our criminal legal system and mass incarceration. So, for example, since the 1980s we've had a steep increase in the number of people who are placed in prisons, in jails.

That means that more people are moving through the court system. So, the approach of the court system has been to center efficiency. They want to move folks into the system as quickly as possible. That requires resources. It's essentially a line of production for incarceration, and our courts are at the heart of it.

Our court system's funding has been steadily increasing to facilitate moving folks more quickly into prison and jail. We should instead be spending money providing mental health clinicians that can assess if someone is even prepared to stand trial, or if they should be receiving mental health support instead.

Those are the ways resources should be used, but instead we're seeing them wasted on incredibly high salaries for law enforcement personnel and judges. I encourage people to Google what the going salaries are for judges in their local county. These are folks that are making an extreme amount of money and are not being held accountable.

A slap on the wrist is often the most that they get when they are in violation of their own internal systems. Too much money is going to people and processes that can't be held accountable.

KOLHATKAR: A lot of folks around the country are increasingly realizing that the highest court in the nation is broken and corrupt. For example, we see corruption on the Supreme Court in terms of Justice Clarence Thomas taking what are essentially bribes and the Court handing down decision after decision that undoes progressive legislation and overturns earlier precedents. This has a very real impact on our lives, from labor rights to LGBTQ+ rights to reproductive rights and more. Do you see that focus on the Supreme Court and its corruption as an opening for a broader discussion on the judiciary as a whole?

ALÉ-FERLITO: Absolutely. One thing that folks should understand is that there are pipelines from the local level all the way up to the Supreme Court which the right wing has been very astute about leveraging for decades. Judges who are serving at the local level may be appointed to a court on the federal level, which may open up the possibility for them to then be appointed to the Supreme Court. There is a prosecutor-to-judge pipeline into local judgeship, into federal judgeship, and ultimately into the Supreme Court.

When we look at the composition of the Supreme Court and its attack on our bodies, particularly for gender-marginalized folks, we can feel powerless. We don't have the power to appoint the Supreme Court justices; the president does. And if the elections didn't go our way as we saw with the administration of Donald Trump, it could open the door for our rights to be rolled back.

KOLHATKAR: And as of this interview, we have three conservative justices that Donald Trump appointed to the US Supreme Court. One third of the court has been appointed by one of the most corrupt presidents in history.

ALÉ-FERLITO: It's mind-boggling how one administration can have such a long-lasting impact on our society.

KOLHATKAR: And they're young judges with lifetime appointments!

ALÉ-FERLITO: Exactly. We need to look at the trajectory of the Supreme Court and our civil liberties not just from what's happening right now, but also in the long term. We're talking about twenty-five to fifty years ahead because that's what the conservatives did. They played the low and slow game. They were covert. They focused on packing courts at every level. We progressives and abolitionists need to start playing the same chess game of disruption of the judiciary.

This summer we're creating a judicial academy for those who are interested in running for judgeship. We will train potential candidates who are underrepresented on the LA County Superior Court how to run and how to be a candidate. We're very excited about that.

We're starting to plant the seeds of what we want to see moving forward. It has to start local. It can start small and still have a big impact. Here in LA County, we are one of the largest—if not the largest—counties in the country with one of the largest law enforcement budgets for our sheriff's department. By investing in changing our local county, we can have reverberating effects, not just in other counties, but at the national level.

I would love to see Judge Holly Hancock appointed to a higher court and to be on the Supreme Court, but ultimately we want to *reduce* the scope and power of the Supreme Court to have material impacts on our lives and our individual freedoms. That is critical because one high-level court should not be stripping an entire nation of people of their civil liberties.

KOLHATKAR: Our court system wasn't made for people like Holly Hancock to take power. If that were to happen, we would see the backlash.

ALÉ-FERLITO: Yes.

KOLHATKAR: What would a world without a judiciary, without policing, without prisons look like for you? That envisioning, that world-building, is such an important part of realizing the hard work to move resources, chip away at power, and eventually abolish these systems that have harmed so many.

ALÉ-FERLITO: Yes, that's such a great question. For me, an abolitionist world is a world that centers everybody's humanity. It's a world that centers the experiences of those most marginalized, that understands that your individual wellness and health and happiness are interconnected with those of everyone around you. The systems in an abolitionist world reflect the values of interconnectivity and interdependence so we don't build things that we have to destroy in the future. An abolitionist world centers the rights, wellness, and sustenance of our environment, alongside the wellness of our individual community members.

9

MELINA ABDULLAH

PARTICIPATORY BUDGETING

Melina Abdullah is a fixture among racial justice activists in Los Angeles, leading Black Lives Matter LA (BLMLA)'s protests and actions from the campus of California State University, Los Angeles, where she's a professor.[34] In 2024, she became Cornel West's choice of vice president for his independent presidential run.[35]

As an outspoken abolitionist, Abdullah has championed defunding the police using a concrete, practical, and deeply democratic method of participatory budgeting where city residents decide how their tax dollars should be spent.

In a conversation in January 2024, Abdullah pointed out how BLMLA was poised to prove that defunding and abolishing police were not impossible. BLMLA's People's Budget survey, conducted prior to the May 2020 police killing of George Floyd, revealed that, when given the opportunity to allocate city funds, most people choose public well-being, health, and safety, rather than law enforcement and punitive measures.[36]

❀ ❀ ❀

SONALI KOLHATKAR: Where did the idea of participatory budgeting come from and was it always a pathway toward reimagining public safety?

MELINA ABDULLAH: Some people think that Black Lives Matter came up with participatory budgeting, that it's some new thing that was developed in order to defund the police. We do want participatory budgeting to be used to defund the police, but the concept goes back many, many decades. It's very deeply rooted in the concept of democracy.

When you talk about participatory budgeting, you're talking about people having an investment in how their tax dollars are spent. And so, rather than having policymakers or elected officials determine without any public input where the dollars go, people actually have a say-so and a voice in where their dollars go.

We know that without the voice of the people, special interests tend to influence local, state, and federal budgets to spend an exorbitant amount—often the lion's share of the budget—on policing and militarism. By special interests, I mean lobby groups like police associations, which are not unions, but which wield tremendous power, as well as defense contractors.

KOLHATKAR: How have participatory budgeting processes been applied toward defunding police in Los Angeles specifically?

ABDULLAH: In 2020, when the COVID-19 pandemic first hit Los Angeles, we started looking around and asked why they were still spending upwards of fifty percent of the city's general fund on police. Nobody was even outdoors. What we needed were resources for people staying in their homes and mental health support. We're still in the midst of the worst public health crisis in global history and need resources to address it. That's where our funds should be going, but upwards of fifty percent of the city's general fund is spent on police. We should be spending money on services, not police.

We convened a meeting with virtually every Black organization in greater Los Angeles, and we all agreed that we wanted to fund services, not police. If we as organizers felt that way, what did Black Los Angeles feel?

To answer that question, we launched the People's Budget survey. What came back was that people's top two funding priorities are mental health and housing. The top two things they wanted to cut funding to were police and traffic enforcement.

Those priorities intensified in May 2020 when there was a worldwide uproar following the state-sanctioned lynching of George Floyd. People started asking: What would police abolition look like? What would new systems of public safety look like? We had collected two to three months of data before Floyd's murder, and then after May 2020, people wanted to defund the police even further. That's what the People's Budget sought to amplify.

Since 2020, we've done that survey every single year. We've organized town hall meetings, workshops, work groups, and focus groups to figure out how we can get to where most people want to be. Black women most intensely want to move away from oppressive models of policing and towards this resource-rich, community-focused system of public safety.

KOLHATKAR: How has the People's Budget been received by elected officials such as the mayor and city councilmembers?

ABDULLAH: Former LA mayor Eric Garcetti refused to receive the People's Budget presentation. We were able to present it to the LA City Council because then–City Council president Herb Wesson invited us to do so. One of the things that we believe cost Herb Wesson his reelection in 2020 was a complete turn in how he viewed public safety. One of his most famous quotes from that time was, "I won't always be an elected official, but I'll always be a Black man, a Black father, and a Black grandfather."

As he ran for his next seat, he actually rejected the endorsement of the Police Protective League and the Association for Los Angeles Deputy Sheriffs. He sent the endorsement back saying, "I don't want it anymore." And we think that probably cost him that seat.

After Floyd was lynched, there was a Black Lives Matter uprising and a period of racial reckoning. In order to kind of appease that movement, many elected officials were willing to hear us out. That year we gave our presentation inside City Council chambers, and it was particularly compelling. By 2021, a backlash had begun, and we weren't invited back by the full city council. We had to push Herb Wesson's successor, Nury Martinez, who we later found out was not a fan of Black people,[37] to allow us into that space to give a presentation.

By 2022, very few elected officials or city councilmembers would hear our presentation. So, city councilmembers who see themselves as allies like Mike Bonin and Marqueece Harris-Dawson were eager to receive that information. When Karen Bass was elected mayor in 2023, we were able to give the People's Budget presentation to the mayor.

The mayor of Los Angeles didn't invite us to City Hall. Instead, she came to our 'hood and our home: the Center for Black Power in Africatown, which some people call Leimert Park, the birthplace of Black Lives Matter. She came there and, before a packed room of hundreds of mostly Black Angelenos, we gave the People's Budget presentation to her.

Unfortunately, when we gave that presentation, it was toward the end of the budget process. So even though she received the information, she'd already gone along with what many advisors told her to do and had, in fact, increased the police budget.

In 2024, we've been invited to present her the results of the survey and the results of the entire People's Budget process earlier in the budget process. We hope that it's considered as she builds the new budget. Hopefully, she'll consider us as deeply as she considers police interests.

KOLHATKAR: Can you put the Los Angeles effort around participatory budgeting into a national context? Is LA further along than other cities? In addition to Minneapolis, we've seen flashpoints in cities like Detroit, Oakland, and Seattle, where there've been efforts to defund the police.

ABDULLAH: Sure. Since 2020, we've been convening with groups located everywhere from Santa Clara, California to Des Moines, Iowa to discuss a People's Budget process. There are now between thirty and fifty cities replicating this process. And there are some groups whose participatory budgeting work predates our own.

It's gaining traction. People, no matter what their political stance, believe in the concept of democracy. They say, "Taxes are *our* money. We should have a say in how they are spent." We're able to get lots of folks on board around that.

In fact, what we see also is that, regardless of political persuasion, people tend to lean toward defunding the police. They may not like that term "defunding" anymore, but when they see a simple pie chart presented to neighborhood councils in Los Angeles, they see in red that fifty-four percent of the city's general fund goes to police. Everybody, from the Howard Jarvis tax people to Black folks in South Central Los Angeles and Watts, knows that's too much money for police.

That's true in Los Angeles, and it's true in Oakland, where I know people like Cat Brooks and the Anti-Police Terror Project are also working toward defunding police. It's also true in Minneapolis, where the organization Black Visions is working on issues like this. These are just a few of the thirty to fifty municipalities that have been part of these People's Budget calls.

KOLHATKAR: When we look at the results of the People's Budget surveys, people were happy to designate a mere 1.64 percent of the entire city's budget to police, which is quite remarkable. As an abolitionist, do you want to see something on that order or zero percent?

ABDULLAH: I say zero! There are very few Black people who feel safer when a police cruiser pulls up behind them in traffic. So, when we think about that, we know intuitively as Black people that police don't keep us safe.

Police rarely prevent crime. They might *respond* to a crime *after* it's happened, but they are only successful in solving the most egregious crimes less than two percent of the time.

We have to do a better job talking about alternative models, particularly ones that have already proven to be successful. Newark, New Jersey, for example, has invested deeply in community safety programs. Phenomenal work is also being done by people like Aqeela Sherrills—cofounder of the Community Based Public Safety Collective in Watts. These efforts have been much, much more successful in making communities safer than policing.

The most brilliant economist that I know, Dr. Julianne Malveaux, says that budgets are moral and ethical documents. If we spend almost $4 billion on police in the city of Los Angeles, that's $4 billion that could have provided housing, healthcare, and mental healthcare for all. We have to be willing to take funding from oppressive forces and invest in the things that actually make us safe.

So, yes, my position is let's completely abolish police and use those funds to invest in forms of public safety and wellness that are rooted in community.

KOLHATKAR: What will it take to spread this idea of participatory budgeting in cities around the country? It's one thing for it to work on a local level. It's another thing to realize that vision nationally. And even though cities like Minneapolis and Oakland are working on defunding, the US is a huge country. Are you hopeful that this idea of deciding budgets in a participatory way is catching on?

ABDULLAH: Yes. People like it, and it's going to catch on. Participatory budgeting is not abolition, but it is one way of pulling masses of people into a process and engaging them in ways that empower communities to radically re-envision and reimagine the world and work towards the world of our greatest hopes and dreams.

IO.

ALICIA GARZA

FROM BLACK HISTORY TO BLACK FUTURES

Alicia Garza will go down in American history as one of the three Black women, alongside Patrisse Cullors and Ayo Tometi, who conceived of and popularized the slogan #BlackLivesMatter in 2013 in response to the acquittal of Trayvon Martin's killer, George Zimmerman.[38] That hashtag went on to frame the 2014 Ferguson uprising[39] and the record-breaking racial justice protests of 2020.[40]

And yet, the question remains: How can this country ensure that Black lives matter today and in the future? Abolitionists imagine a world where cooperation, community, justice, and solidarity form the heart of an equitable multi-racial democracy.

Visions of such a future are central to Garza's work with the Black Futures Lab and Black to the Future Action Fund. "Black communities have always been futurists," she says. What that means is that "because of the way that the rules have been rigged against our communities, we've been forced to imagine a new future with possibilities for freedom."

Working during and between elections, Garza is leading efforts to ensure that grassroots groups are properly resourced to engage and mobilize Black voters, as well as train a new generation of individual organizers. In an interview in January 2023, she discussed the work it takes to realize a just future for Black people.

SONALI KOLHATKAR: Tell me about the organizations that you are the principal of—the Black Futures Lab and Black to the Future Action Fund—and specifically the work that these organizations embarked on after the 2022 midterm elections to infuse Black-led voting rights organizations around the country with the financial resources that they need.

ALICIA GARZA: We established the Black Organizing Innovations Program because every election cycle we lament and wring our hands about how Black communities are underengaged or engaged at the last minute. And so, every single cycle people get confused and concerned about how Black people are going to participate and whether or not Black people are going to participate. Our program intervenes in this cycle.

Black communities participate in elections at higher levels than many other racial or ethnic groups because Black communities have a lot at stake and a lot on the line. We invest in organizations and are there every single step of the way to encourage and help germinate Black political participation and year-round activation of Black communities, not just during election cycles.

With the Black Organizing Innovations Program, we are resourcing creative ways to keep our communities engaged between election cycles. What we know and what we believe is that infusing those organizations and those strategies with resources to keep our communities engaged will play out better for us in the next election cycle.

Research shows that when Black communities are engaged early and all the time, we will participate in elections. And so, we encourage that participation by resourcing the work that it takes to be the glue between election cycles.

KOLHATKAR: You partnered with the organization Black Voters Matter, which has been one of the most important on-the-ground voter mobilization projects in the South. Why did you choose this organization and what did they do with the funding?

GARZA: Organizations like Black Voters Matter have been deeply underfunded to do the work that our country depends on to keep Black communities engaged. So, we gratefully and happily moved resources to that organization and partnered with them to get people involved, excited about voting, and looking future-forward.

We had people taking the Black Census to let us know about what their policy priorities were moving into 2023 and, of course, in upcoming cycles where we'll be deciding who leads this nation. We're hoping that more partnerships like that can and will happen through the Black Innovations Organizing Project.

We are resourcing organizations throughout the South, throughout the Midwest, and a couple in California to do that necessary work, to keep our communities engaged in the process of democracy. Democracy doesn't begin or end with casting your vote. Democracy is a project that needs to ensure that all of our communities are responsible for what happens in the state legislatures and in the White House. In order to do that, we need to make sure that our communities are being engaged consistently. And we need to make sure that our communities' priorities are being heard.

KOLHATKAR: Tell me more about the Black Census project. It sounds very ambitious.

GARZA: That's right. We launched the Black Census project

in 2018, and it's currently the largest survey of Black people in America since Reconstruction. It was the very first program of the Black Futures Lab, and the goal of it was to better understand, from Black communities ourselves, what we were experiencing every single day in relationship to the economy, our democracy, and our society. We also research the biggest problems of our generation and what solutions Black communities want to develop in response.

We take those solutions, and we turn them into policy that works for our communities. We then work to get that policy passed in cities and states across the country. What we know now, going into another interesting political era, is that Black communities are again being undercounted and underengaged. This has devastating consequences for whether public policy is, in fact, public. Meaning, does public policy reflect the needs, concerns, and experiences of Black communities who disproportionately feel the negative impacts of public policy that does not address our needs?

We relaunched the Black Census project with the goal of becoming the largest survey of Black people in American history. And we are well on our way. We are collecting 200,000 responses to the Black Census project and using the data to inform our legislative priorities going into the 2024 election cycle.

KOLHATKAR: What sorts of questions are being asked in the Black Census?

GARZA: Well, here's what's so great about the Black Census project. Number one, it's a nonpartisan survey. We're looking for responses from Black people from every position on the political spectrum, not just people who agree with us. You don't have to be an activist. You don't have to be somebody who believes in social justice. We want to better understand the needs, experiences, and priorities of all Black people in America, not just US citizens. We want your voice to be heard.

The other thing that's really important about the Black Census project is that you don't have to give any of your personal information to participate. People are rightfully concerned about where their personal information will go, whether or not it's going to get sold to somebody they don't want it to go to. We don't require you to give us that information in order to have your voice heard and your needs prioritized. Whether or not you opt in to engage in campaigns is up to you.

The purpose of the Black Census, however, is to offer opportunities for you to be a part of solutions. We don't just collect data. We want to make that data live and be in service of transforming your everyday life for the better. What that means for us is working with partners to run policy campaigns in cities and states across the nation that change the conditions of Black communities and change the rules regarding how these communities participate and are resourced.

KOLHATKAR: Let's talk about how individual organizers are being trained and why that's important. The Black to the Future Public Policy Institute has graduated almost 100 Black organizers. Tell me about this aspect of the organizing work that is necessary to have a sort of multispectrum approach to elections, democracy, and voting.

GARZA: The reason that we started the Black Public Policy Institute at the Black to the Future Action Fund and the Black Futures Lab is because we want our communities to be equipped with the tools that we need to make the rules and change the rules. At the end of the day, when we think about laws and policies that impact our lives, most of the time our communities are not involved in the development of those processes, but we certainly are impacted by them. We want to change that equation. Black communities deserve to be the people who are making the rules and changing the rules that shape our daily lives.

We offer an eight-month policy fellowship for Black organizers to learn how to write, win, and implement new rules in cities and states across the nation. It's not a program where you just get a training booklet and then you're sent off with a certificate. We train you to design the policies that communities want to see enacted, and we help support you through an actual legislative cycle to get that policy passed.

And we've been successful. In places like California, we worked with the Young Women's Freedom Center to make sure that we changed the rules about sentencing guidelines for young women who were coerced into committing crimes as a result of being in a domestic violence partnership or an intimate partner violence partnership. We want to make sure that the needs of our communities are being addressed, and that's a great example of how we do that.

The program is rigorous. It's not something that you have to do on your own time, on your own dime. The goal is to build the capacity of organizations to learn and know how to make the rules and change the rules that are impacting families and communities across the nation.

The other thing that is so important about this program is that you get mentorship from experts who are policy advocates and know how to do the things that we're trying to train you in, particularly in your area of expertise.

The final thing that is so awesome about this program is that it's really Black! We have Black trainers. We have Black participants. We are using the experiences and the cultural competency of Black communities to train our communities to succeed. It's a very unique program, and we're so honored to be able to offer it to our communities. We're already seeing the results, and we're deeply grateful and humbled to everyone who has trusted us with this process.

The eighty-plus fellows who have graduated have given us incredible feedback about how important the program is, not just for individuals, but for building the ecosystem and infrastructure in our communities to be more powerful politically.

KOLHATKAR: How do you link history to the future? What are the most important lessons that you take from Black history as you envision a just future?

GARZA: One of the most important things that I take from Black history is that Black communities have always been futurists. Because of the way that the rules have been rigged against our communities, we've been forced to imagine a future with new possibilities for freedom.

And that's why each February, during Black History Month, the Black Futures Lab spends our time focusing on the future. We take lessons from the past. We take experiences from the present. We reimagine what our futures can and should look like, with all of us working together towards a common goal.

Black History Month, which I like to think of as Black Futures Month, offers us the opportunity to reimagine a just society, a just democracy, and a just economy, where everyone has what they need to thrive, and nobody gets left behind because of our race, gender, sexuality, disability, or immigration status. All Black people deserve to be powerful in every single aspect of our lives. Focusing on the future during Black History Month is an opportunity for us to reflect on the work that we've done thus far to get us there and the work that we still need to do to keep us going.

KOLHATKAR: When we think about how organizing happens today versus twenty, thirty, or fifty years ago, we do live in a very different world, and yet, of course, there are things that are the same. The biggest difference is digital technology, which has upsides and downsides. How do you harness the best of technology to ensure that those things that people were fighting for fifty years ago can still be realized using these new tools?

GARZA: I think the trick is to make sure that what stays consistent, across generations and across eras of organizing, is the building of personal relationships. What we know about organizing in the 1930s, in the 1940s and organizing in the 2000s, the 2010s, and the 2020s is that organizing and moving something together requires relationships.

Technology allows us to build relationships across physical and geographical barriers, but community organizing still requires presence. You cannot meme your way to justice. The path forward requires that we know each other, that we're connected, that we know that we depend on each other to survive.

It's important, therefore, for us to remember to nurture the face-to-face relationship-building aspect of our work. Screens and technology can sometimes help facilitate bringing together people that wouldn't be able to do so otherwise. But we have to make sure that there's other work that's happening to deepen those relationships beyond the screens, beyond the hashtags, and beyond the memes.

KOLHATKAR: When the 2020 racial justice uprisings happened, people began paying attention to racist police violence. But organizers like yourself who had been active for many years put that into a broader context of what freedom means, and it's not just freedom from police brutality.

And yet, Black people are still getting killed by police. More Americans were killed by police in 2022 than any year before that. It was a record-breaking year for police killings. Why has greater public attention seemingly not had an impact on even just this one critical aspect, which is racist police brutality?

GARZA: I would argue that it has had an impact, just not enough. Reckonings happen in cycles, and the racial reckoning that began in 2020 is far from complete.

Achieving racial justice cannot just be symbolic. Putting up signs in our windows, posting a hashtag, and blacking out our profile pictures help express our outrage, but are not enough to change laws. When police commit crimes in our communities, we must hold them accountable. Reimagining public safety and divesting resources from policing are important, but achieving the goal of racial justice requires more.

Getting to racial justice means making sure that people have the things that they need to survive and thrive. Getting to racial justice means making sure that the rules are applied evenly in governing, policing, and across the board.

Getting to racial justice means not allowing for unequal outcomes based on race, gender, sexuality, disability, or citizenship status, among other things. We have to enact policies, change rules, and hold people accountable in order to reach the goals that we seek. Achieving racial justice is an ongoing project that we cannot afford to abandon.

II

LEAH PENNIMAN

ABOLITION VIA FOOD JUSTICE

When discussing police, courts, and prisons, the topics of food justice and land ownership might seem unrelated. But educator and food justice activist Leah Penniman, who runs Soul Fire Farm in upstate New York, sees them as intimately linked.

Penniman, who authored the acclaimed book *Farming While Black*, sees our current corporatized food system as violent and our food and land as incarcerated.

When envisioning what a society without police and prisons could look like, Penniman asks us to imagine restoring people's deep connections to land and growing our own food. She challenges us to ask the question, what if we decarcerated our people and our food simultaneously, relying on the life-giving possibilities of land stewardship while rejecting the death-making institutions of policing and imprisonment?

In a wide-ranging interview in January 2024, Penniman addressed such possibilities, seeing them as critical to an abolition-based vision of the world.

❋ ❋ ❋

SONALI KOLHATKAR: This country has historically discriminated against Black farmers and disproportionately advantaged white farmers and white-run agricultural corporations. Why is connecting people, especially Black people, to land so important for you?

LEAH PENNIMAN: As Malcolm X said, land is "the basis of freedom, justice and equality." In this country, land ownership, as you mentioned, is so skewed that ninety-eight percent of the agricultural land value is in white hands. This is not because Black and Brown folks aren't interested in farming. We have a waiting list around the block for our farmer training programs and most of those farmers are landless. It's because of a history of genocidal violence against Indigenous people, chattel slavery in all its permutations, sharecropping, and convict leasing. It's because of our own government's discrimination against Black farmers and the land grabbing that's going on now under the guise of corporate profit.

We have a situation where our access to land is slipping away. This creates a crisis because land is not only the basis of freedom but of cultural belonging, intergenerational wealth, and our capacity to feed ourselves, build homes, and have a place to have family reunions and bury our dead together. We came so close to being able to regain some of that through the Justice for Black Farmers Act and the efforts to reform the US Department of Agriculture (USDA). The lawsuits that white farmers brought, claiming "reverse racism," have really slowed down those gains that were promised from 2020–2022.

But we're not giving up, and right now it really is up to the grassroots. We're seeing how much the connection to land, when it's rooted in choice, not only allows people to think about a way of making a living that is rooted in the Buddhist concept of "right livelihood" and support of their community, but starts to heal that generational trauma and gives folks a taste of a world that's possible, that's connected to our heritage, to the Earth, and to our own dignity.

KOLHATKAR: How do you link the abolition of police, prisons, and the entire criminal justice system to food justice?

PENNIMAN: It's so important because a lot of folks, when they think about these systems of state violence, police, and prisons, don't understand how it's intersectional with other issues. One of the most powerful illustrations I saw of this was a Geographic Information System (GIS) map overlay of New York City neighborhoods that were the most heavily policed. These were areas with the highest rates of incarceration in the city and were the very same neighborhoods with low rates of Black home ownership, lower educational quality, lower access to fresh fruits and vegetables—essentially food-apartheid neighborhoods.

It's not an accident of history that these very same zip codes that are criminalized and overpoliced are the neighborhoods where people don't have access to fresh food, clean water, and fresh air. These are the same neighborhoods where factories and waste sites are located. It's all part of a larger history of racialized discrimination and environmental injustice.

The beautiful thing about bringing abolition into the conversation is that it forces us to widen our lens and ask: What are the underlying causes of these systemic racial oppressions?

We have to look at racial capitalism. We have to look at settler colonialism. We have to look at the ways that Black bodies have been seen as only useful for profit, including the profit of private prisons, and the way that land and autonomy have been taken away from Black and Brown communities. Seeing through the lens of racial capitalism allows us to get at root causes.

Abolition speaks to the beautiful and important yearning that we have for nonviolent liberation. In the long march to liberation, we don't want to be replicating the kinds of structures of violence that caused the problems in the first place. We don't want to be policing one another. We don't want to be imposing our will on other humans or on the Earth in ways that are non-consensual. We don't want to use coercion and force in order to live.

When we look at the food system right now, it's very much based on violent coercion. It's based on the exploitation of farm workers who are often displaced from their homelands because of so-called free trade agreements, war, economic desperation, or unfair immigration policy.

Under racial capitalism, land is treated as nothing more than a natural resource to be extracted, and violence is committed against the climate and the waters. And so, when we frame abolition as a yearning for nonviolent liberation, we also have to ask ourselves: In our work, how do we embody democracy, consent, dignity, care, mutual care, and loving kindness? This is very inspiring to me and something that I see as a powerful impulse in the rising generation of farmers.

KOLHATKAR: What happens when young folks, especially young people of color, and specifically Black youth, first experience farming in spaces like Soul Fire Farm?

PENNIMAN: It's been really powerful. My spouse and I came out here in 2006 with our young children to this rocky mountain and expected to be quite alone. We had resigned ourselves to that because we had bought into this myth that Black and Brown folks were so traumatized by land-based oppression that there wasn't an interest in returning to an undignified way of being on the land.

So, it was a shock to me as much as it was to anyone else that, after we officially opened our farm in 2010 and started to get out there doing our youth programs and feeding the community with doorstep delivery, phone calls were coming in from folks who were interested in being trained.

Then things snowballed. One program turned into two; two turned into eight; ten people coming in a year turned into 2,000. My background is in environmental science, biology, and chemistry, and so I can do a pretty mean class on soil chemistry with cation-exchange capacity and binding sites[41] and feel really good about that.

But the thing that people are taking away in addition to these hard skills, and that they comment on so often, is this immense healing power that comes with being in touch with the land in community with other Black and Brown folks. There is a lineage—a proud agrarian heritage—where we can see the contributions of folks like Dr. George Washington Carver in our understanding of cover cropping and the contributions of Fannie Lou Hamer in our understanding of cooperatives and the relationship of food to liberation.

And so, folks are saying that this contact with the earth and heritage is allowing them to wake up to a future they didn't imagine was possible. It is allowing them to see beyond the harmful relationship they might be in; or the undignified job they might be in; or the narrative they might have bought into that their only future is as a consumer, a sort of a cog in this machine, to saying "maybe it is possible to envision a livelihood, a way of being, that is nourishing to both myself and community." And how people heal and open up to the possibility of what land offers is consistently profound.

KOLHATKAR: Can you give me some examples of people whose lives have been transformed by farming and food justice in ways that they just didn't expect?

PENNIMAN: Sure. And I think that there are so many forces at play. At Soul Fire Farm, we don't want to take undue credit. Folks, ancestors, and communities of lineages are all in play, including the land herself. But it's been amazing to see the alumni from our program take the seeds of what they learned here and plant them in the fertile soils of their homes.

I can think of Catatumbo Cooperative in Chicago, a femme, immigrant, queer co-op that was growing food and feeding folks through the pandemic so beautifully. I admire them so much.

There is also the Shelterwood Collective in the Pacific Northwest that's collectively reindigenizing forest management on hundreds of acres and centering disability justice.

There are folks in the Southeast, outside of Georgia at High Hog Farm, who are reclaiming Black folks' connection to fiber, which has been really severed after the trauma of cotton picking. They are growing both plant and animal fibers, learning and teaching dyeing, spinning, and weaving, and bringing these arts back to life in their community.

We like to think of the Soul Fire network as one tree in a beautiful mycelial superorganism. Our job as one tree in the network is to share our resources and knowledge to other trees in the forest. They then use those resources to express in their own unique, locally adapted way what it looks like to have a beautifully nonviolent, liberatory effort towards food and land justice.

KOLHATKAR: How has racial capitalism perverted and subverted our connection to food? How do we transform that corporatized system of food monopolies, and how does that transformation naturally go hand in hand with a world without prisons and police?

PENNIMAN: Oh, that's such a big question. As you noted, the food system is essentially incarcerated in corporate racial capitalism. As a result, our seed diversity has been decimated. The land is concentrated in the hands of one racial group, and many of those landowners are corporatized at this point. We have workers who are not protected under federal labor laws such as the National Labor Relations Act or the Fair Labor Standards Act. We have consumers who are getting products that are devoid of rich nutrients. The products are processed from crops grown in soils that are overladen with chemicals and then transported over long distances.

There's a huge disconnect between what's on our plate and our own understanding and experience of nourishment. As a result, there is an epidemic of reduced life expectancy, diabetes, heart disease, kidney failure, and other illnesses of the body—and arguably the spirit—that are connected to not having access to wholesome life-giving food.

It's a really big problem. The thing that gives me some hope is remembering that in the long march of history, the incarceration of the food system is only a few hundred years old. Anything that humans can cook up within a few generations, however harmful, could hopefully be dismantled within the same amount of time.

It will take policy changes. Right now, we incentivize trashing the planet and human lives. You have to jump through hoops and get certified to have your food labeled as organic, but you can go ahead and feel free to decimate ecosystems without applying for permission to do so. We need to really think about what we're incentivizing in terms of policy. For example, all fruits and vegetables are relegated to this tiny sliver of the USDA budget called specialty crops, even though they should be at least half of our diets.

The Farm Bill defines specialty crops as "fruits and vegetables, tree nuts, dried fruits, horticulture, and nursery crops (including floriculture)." In 2018, less than half a percent of Farm Bill funding went to the Horticulture title, which is one of twelve sections or titles and where most funding for specialty crop and organic growers comes from.

Five percent of funding went to the Commodity title, which gives direct price and income supports to producers of "staple" commodities like corn, soy, and wheat. These producers, as well as meat producers, also benefit from the Crop Insurance title, which accounted for eight percent of Farm Bill funding. Smaller and specialty crop farmers can be eligible for funding through this title but it works far better for commodity growers, who use up the bulk of its resources.

When we look at land and workers, we're really advocating for wholesale land reform: returning land to native folks; making land available to Black and Brown communities affordably so that we are not just laborers on a corporate farm, but are in a position of management or collective and cooperative owner-ship; and prioritizing what our communities most need. It'll take political pressure, and it will also take good old-fashioned grassroots alternative institution building to realize this.

In some ways, it was really beautiful to see in the pandemic how well-placed some of these small, independent mutual aid networks and co-ops were to be able to pivot and meet the needs of communities. At that same time, the corporatized infra-structure was really unable to change course at the rate that was needed in order to feed our communities.

It was this little glimmer of possibility that showed that this community-created infrastructure is resilient, flexible, adaptable, and can meet our needs. So, I hold on to hope, even though clearly the trend has been to corporatize and to make the food system more violent in the West.

KOLHATKAR: If the incarceration of land is linked to the incarceration of people, then conversely does the decarceration of land and people need to go hand in hand?

PENNIMAN: Absolutely and quite literally. That nasty little loophole in the Thirteenth Amendment that allows slavery in the case where someone has committed a crime (as defined by the courts these days) means that disproportionately Black folks who are incarcerated can be forced to work for no pay.

We see this in fighting the wildfires in California and the West. We saw this during the pandemic with labor shortages in the fields, with folks coming from prison and picking vegetables and grains in order to keep the food system running. We see this with furniture companies and all kinds of corporate entities taking advantage of slave labor legally provided by the Thirteenth Amendment.

Freeing the lands in the food system is a metaphor. But also, quite literally, these systems are intertwined. The prison industrial complex is invested in a corporatized and violent food system.

KOLHATKAR: Incarceration, segregation, and slavery broke up communities and families and severed people's ties with the land as well. Meanwhile, the benefits for white farmers, such as disproportionate access to land, is a way to maintain generational wealth, a way for them to pass wealth down to their descendants. But if we start to rethink food justice and land justice, do we need to also rethink the idea of wealth, money, and capitalism? Do we need new visions to replace the idea of land as money and wealth?

PENNIMAN: Oh, that's beautifully complex, right? We know that hundreds of billions of dollars at a minimum were lost to Black communities through land loss. This was not a voluntary relinquishing of the land. Folks weren't paying for their land, but we had an internal refugee crisis in the early 1900s when Black farmers were at the peak of their land ownership with about 16 million acres.

Then there was a backlash from white supremacists in the South who wanted Black people to stay on the plantation as sharecroppers. Lynchings, arson, and threats drove people off their land. These forces were a major push factor in the Great Migration, which displaced 60 million Black folks to the North, to the West, and to urban areas. The reverberations of that are still being felt psycho-spiritually and economically, with that intergenerational wealth being lost, while at the same time, intergenerational wealth has accumulated unabated in white communities.

There certainly are whole sectors of Black food-justice communities that are very much advocating for intergenerational wealth, including the wealth of the land, and finance vehicles for that. There are also factions within the Black land justice community that are saying that thinking about land from a monetary framework is inherently problematic.

So, how do we demonetize land? How do we think about collective and cooperative land stewardship versus ownership? What are the ways we can use the white man's tools of land trusts, co-ops, easements, B-Corps, and those sorts of structures to soften the enclosure and private property orientation of law in this country?

At Soul Fire Farm, we tend to fall a bit in the latter camp where our land is held cooperatively, and we do a lot of organizing with the Indigenous Mohican Nation around land return and shared sovereignty. We've made it so that it would be quite difficult to ever make any money from selling our land. Lawyers throw their hands up at this, not understanding why we want to muck up our title.

At the same time, it would be unfair to say, "Well, white folks get to accumulate all this wealth, and Black folks are obligated somehow to think differently about it," right? So, it's a very complex issue.

KOLHATKAR: Do the connections between Black and Indigenous communities inform a lot of your thinking around food justice and farming?

PENNIMAN: Yes. I think it's impossible for any one community to get free by ourselves. These multiethnic, multiracial coalitions are crucial for us. We think that the Indigenous communities globally who are closest to the land and the earth have the wisdom we need to chart the way forward. That includes African Indigenous folks, Turtle Island Indigenous folks, Asian Indigenous folks. We have spent a lot of time and resources building those coalitions. We're a member of Via Campesina and work internationally in these *intercambios*—exchanges of ideas.

We're also accountable to the people upon whose land we live and work, and that's the Mohican Nation. For the past several years, we've built a friendship with the Stockbridge-Munsee Band of Mohicans, who are predominantly located in Wisconsin and have worked on seed rematriation projects, interrupting a pipeline development project that would have desecrated a sacred historical site and a 250-acre land-return project.

There's a lot going on there, and it's very important to us. We don't see any contradiction in working for Black land sovereignty and liberation while holding deep solidarity with and commitment to Native liberation and Native land sovereignty.

GINA DENT

DOING ABOLITION EVERYWHERE

Having an abolition mindset isn't just relegated to the criminal justice system. It means reimagining society as a whole, especially in how we think about our responsibilities to one another while balancing our individual rights. This balance is one of many abolition-related ideas that Gina Dent thinks about.

Dent has spent years alongside the godmother of abolition, Angela Davis, in exploring how abolition ideals intersect with feminism and social justice movements. She codirects the Visualizing Abolition project at the University of California, Santa Cruz, where she is a Feminist Studies professor. The project challenges narratives that link prisons to justice and imagines new ways of thinking about a prison-free future. She has also published a conversation with Angela Davis titled "Prison as a Border," and is coauthor with Davis, Erica Meiners, and Beth Richie of the book *Abolition. Feminism. Now.* Dent has accumulated deep wisdom on how to put abolition ideals into practice. A January 2024 interview I did with Dent is a fitting conclusion to this book.

❀ ❀ ❀

SONALI KOLHATKAR: Abolition entered the national dialogue during and after the uprisings of 2020. Was that year a game changer for policing and prisons, or have they maintained their status as "necessary" parts of society?

GINA DENT: I don't know if I would say that moment was the game changer. I think what preceded that moment, that made us ready for that moment, was the game changer: decades of work toward abolition, specifically prison abolition. Those years of organizing are what allowed us to take advantage of that moment, be prepared for that moment, and know how to respond in that moment. The degree of sophistication that people had when they were asked about the viability of a society that operated without prisons and policing was really astonishing.

I think what transformed in that time period was a relationship to policing rather than only imprisonment. The movement that I had been involved with previously was much more focused on the hidden aspects of our carceral system and less focused on things that were already being handled by another wing of the movement around stop-and-frisk, or driving while Black, or the racial differences in the rates of arrest, the treatment after arrest, et cetera—all that kind of work that people have been doing for a very long time. What was really new at that moment was the way that abolition became an all-encompassing approach to addressing the carceral system.

We have continued to stay in that moment, though I know many municipalities are still struggling with new ways to organize society. We are not done with that.

KOLHATKAR: You have specifically written about abolition's links to feminism alongside Angela Davis. The two of you pointed out that feminism cannot be attached to incarceration, that feminism has to be anti-racist and anti-capitalist. How does feminism need to redefine itself in a post-abolition world?

DENT: I guess I'd put it slightly differently. Angela Davis, Erica Meiners, Beth Richie and I have all been involved in the abolitionist movement in different ways for a long time. We really saw the need to address the problem of not thinking about abolition when doing feminist work, specifically against domestic violence and other forms of interpersonal violence.

That doesn't mean we can wait until abolition to transform our feminism. It really means that our work needs to be *both* abolitionist and feminist. And so, we use the compound noun "abolition feminism" to underscore that idea. We strongly believe that separating abolition and feminism does violence to our movements.

It's important to balance the need to address harm caused by the state and private harm caused on the interpersonal level. We need to develop a society that changes our relationships to each other and how we deal with both sources of harm. It's not something that can be thought about in an additive way—abolition plus feminism—or even something that we could address ex post facto.

KOLHATKAR: There was a time when the term "restorative justice" was very trendy. Is that idea or term still relevant in as much as we can apply it to harm reduction and interpersonal violence?

DENT: "Restorative justice" is a term that I sometimes hear used interchangeably with other terms within the abolitionist movement. I live in Oakland, California, home to an organization called Restorative Justice for Oakland Youth, whose work I have followed for a long time. Some part of that work would probably be considered abolitionist, and some part of that work might be in another arena. I've heard people use the term restorative justice in so many contexts.

Restorative justice has sometimes been tricky in the sense that it was built first on cultural practices that were white and not necessarily anti-racist—Quaker and Christian—and then later on practices extrapolated from Indigenous and African communities. I think those things might work well in communities where a cultural connection to those practices and ideas is strong, but I think it's hard to move those same practices into every environment, especially without considering their origins and histories more carefully.

I prefer to use the term "transformative justice," and also to attend to "transitional justice" for frameworks that are more global, but I'm less concerned about the actual labels that people use when they're doing this kind of work. I'm more concerned with evaluating how much the organizations are moving us toward or away from carcerality.

KOLHATKAR: I think a lot of people who identify with the tenets of abolition still feel like they need concrete examples of what that could look like when harm is done. If we don't rely on policing, courts, and prisons, what *do* we rely on? I know that there's much to be said in terms of how we reduce harms by funding the things that keep us safe to begin with. But of course, we can't completely eradicate harm by fully funding all the things that we need. So, what might the nuts and bolts of a new system look like?

DENT: Many people in the movement have argued that we already have a lot of the nuts and bolts. It's not as if we're going to build a completely new society at once. We're trying to revitalize practices that are equitable, healing, and where our interpersonal relationships are not dependent on racial hierarchies, gender hierarchies, and certainly not on class hierarchies—which may be the most important one to draw out. Those ways of thinking deeply about social inequities and reaching for a way of embracing all people are fundamental to what it means to build toward abolition.

We already have some of those practices, and people are doing this work in local spaces, and that's so exciting to see. Unfortunately, capitalist media invisibilize abolitionist stories that encourage us to imagine how we could live together differently. Thus, it's important for those involved in these organizations and communities to keep telling the stories of what's happening.

I don't know anyone in the abolitionist movement who is naive about harms or violence. In fact, most of us are survivors of some form of violence. Many people come to the movement because they're so dissatisfied with what they find once they confront the criminal legal system. In *Abolition. Feminism. Now.,* Angela Davis, Erica Meiners, Beth Richie, and I focus especially on gender violence. We examine the ways that people are often disappointed when they have been harmed and then try and process what happened while being further harmed by our "justice" system.

As they're being poked and prodded and asked to recount what happened, they are forced to see what has happened to them and what the perpetrator has done in individualistic rather than systemic terms. Those things feel very unsatisfying for people who are survivors of violence. As a result, we are driven to develop other ways to cope with that violence, to repair relationships and communities, and to build toward prevention through non-carceral frameworks.

We're not saying that violence will immediately go away. I don't think any of us are imagining a future free of harms. There might be different harms and patterns, and there will probably be people who are more vulnerable than others. As we study the past, we find that some supposed advancements—reforms—often result in unanticipated further harms. That's why addressing gender violence carries important lessons for the whole abolitionist movement. Equal treatment models that measure the status of women and gender nonconforming people, for example, through the length of prison sentences of perpe-trators or the criminalization of further behaviors have fueled incarceration rates in their usual pattern. And that pattern of incarceration doubles down on the inequities created through racial capitalism, so that in seeking to address some harm through a carceral grammar, we have created further harms.

It's not to say there wouldn't be consequences in response to harm. The question is, do those consequences actually help build a healthier society, or do those consequences invisibilize the problem and produce further violence? By that I mean the violence of incarceration and punishment that has no actual capacity to help people to rebuild their lives. Those ways of han-dling the problems continue to feed and reinforce, not diminish, the problem of violence.

Prison is not a place that solves violence. Prison is a place that replicates and even reorganizes that violence and extends it out into the communities around prisons—not only through those who are released (the most obvious assumption that furthers criminalization of some) but through the relationships that the prison industrial complex organizes.

In addition to the harms that people describe when they use the term "violent crimes," there's also the violence of not being able to make a good life when a person has completed their sentence, the violence of continually being perceived as a felon or a criminal and denied things that a person without a record can enjoy.

Abolition feminists work at the practices of care that build on the forms of collectivity that are very fragile and discouraged in our societies, but that we nonetheless have. For example, many of us are reaching for practices that have been described through Indigenous communities. Not to romanticize them, not to decontextualize them from their histories and their own hierar-chical practices, and not to extract them from the larger cultural fabric, but to continue to learn, think through, compare, and practice what it means to create a different relationship to land, to territory, to property, and to capital.

KOLHATKAR: How do we bring about a widespread shift where we start to embrace the idea of collective liberation, collective responsibility, and the restoration of people and society?

DENT: It's ongoing, but under the conditions of racial capitalism and neoliberalism, it's challenging. This reminds me of the distinction between what have been described as responsibility-based cultures and rights-based cultures.

One of the most interesting sets of discussions that I tend to have, especially with young organizers, has to do with their sense of their right to things, such as the right to be free from harm. Sometimes this comes up even in organizational conversations and struggles. Instead, I am drawn to formations that try to reorient us toward the question of what our responsibilities to each other are.

One way of imagining what this might be like is the analogy to wearing a medical mask during a pandemic. What does it say about a culture where an individual's right to be mask-free is prioritized over a collective responsibility to protect others during a pandemic? It's not a perfect example, but I think the analogy allows us to see that we need to be much more responsibility-based in our way of understanding our lives. Conversations around self-care can be productively complicated when we discuss, for example, how much formerly incarcerated folks who work in the movement after their release tend to find deep meaning and connection. I've heard time and again about how much being able to do that work is connected to a feeling of greater wellness. These are small, but not inconsequential, adjustments to how we think of thriving.

Even in terms of activism, questions as to who is represented as a leader or who are the central organizers come up a lot. This was a strong focus in the phase before 2020. Black Lives Matter activists and other people were talking in a different way, sometimes through Black feminism, and sometimes for other reasons, about what it means to be *leaderful* rather than relying on charismatic leaders. Yet, we have continued to see how intractable this problem can be and how it has been a force in the attempted undoing of that very movement.

We need to move away from a culture that reinforces individualism, especially through its carceral logics. I teach legal studies and work on these issues, often with people in college and graduate school. I often describe what I refer to as the "love of the law"—the way that even those who are activists and involved in abolition imagine the legal system as the fix for itself.

I'm not saying that I don't work with many lawyers, as well as legal scholars, who make necessary and incredible contributions that the movement could never do without. That's not my point. In fact, those practitioners are often most aware of the limitations of our legal system. The point is that there is a kind of belief and faith in law—a desire to constantly create new laws or revise and reform other laws, and not to attend to the accretion of laws that build on and strengthen the same foundation. I think "breaking up with law" is important, which is part of the real threat of actual Critical Race Theory, a school of legal reasoning that contests the ahistoricism in US jurisprudence.

Our "love of the law" is reinforced constantly, not primarily because of our experience with the actual legal system but because of how it, especially the criminal legal system, is consistently and constantly represented to us. Or rather, the way that the law is represented *is* our experience of it. Being able to represent it differently is important to the project of abolition— hence the deep work on language that has led to replacing the terms "prisoner" and "justice system" and the introduction of concepts such as the prison industrial complex.

The main project I've been engaged with for many years addresses issues of visuality, how the carceral system is naturalized for us, and how we are continually taught to rely on it as it's the only thing we can imagine.

If you think about the fact that we have no moving visual cultural history without the presence of the prison inside of it—early film, so much of it focused on criminality and incarceration—we don't have a way of even imagining how we could live without these structures. We need to pay attention to all of the ways in which that dependency is constructed and reinforced.

We have to do the cultural work of creating other ways of thinking about abolition. That can mean moving away from yet another focus on the conditions of imprisonment or from trying to convince people how horrible prisons are. I think most people have a sense of that already. But what they don't know is how to get away from the system that we have, how to move towards something different, how to even imagine what that might look like, because we're always making small adjustments in terms of what we think would create a more just system—reforms. We're not actually thinking about reorganizing our relationships to one another and the harms that occur between us, but that's what we need to do.

KOLHATKAR: Are you hopeful that a new, younger generation of Americans, particularly Black and Brown youth, are taking the torch on abolition, learning from earlier generations, who learned from generations before them, to reimagine our entire society?

DENT: Because of my work and organizing, I am with younger people a lot, and I'm very impressed with their commitments. Some of the commitments extend from their disappointments, and some of those disappointments are catastrophic. For example, look at climate change, where younger people know that it's an emergency and know that we have to work together differently.

Sometimes that energy is still focused on the negative, on what we have to tear down. But the focus of abolition is to build, reinforce, and reclaim. *That* is the additional work that will allow us to really make a transition.

What does it mean to infuse all of our organizations, workspaces, play spaces, and educational spaces with abolitionist principles? It doesn't just mean taking the police out of schools. Though that's an important start—you can't really imagine that you're treating the problems between young people by suspending them or locking them up.

But we also need to imagine new ways of organizing schools. What are the topics that are going to be researched? What are the things that are going to be shared? What are the ways the classroom will be organized? Who are the teachers? Do we have a universal design in our curriculum that allows everyone to participate? What does relevance mean in a curriculum? There are so many ways that abolition requires us to rethink all of our different ways of interacting with each other.

I know that sounds very overwhelming, but it can also be quite simple and concrete. I happen to be speaking from a particular place right now at the University of California, Santa Cruz, where we have a project called Visualizing Abolition at the Institute of the Arts and Sciences. And it is a regular part of our practice to think about these issues in terms of staffing, in terms of how we organize events, in terms of why we offer food and who we share the food with during as well as when we finish an event, and all of the things that make a caring space beyond just making sure that the externally focused public events are feeding people's questions, and intellectually giving people something to think about and to imagine.

It is possible for us to be doing that work every day in every place we are. Abolitionist work is not only happening in abolitionist organizations. Those are important and we want to sustain them, and if there's one close to you, join it, or you could try to create one. But, also, it's important for us to be doing this work everywhere we are.

CONCLUSION

TRANSFORMATION

Dortell Williams has been incarcerated for more than three decades and will remain so indefinitely. At the young age of twenty-three, he was convicted of the murder of his wife through the ambiguous charge of "lying in wait." Police described him as a gang member even though he had never been in a gang. What better way to condemn a Black person than using a racist stereotype? Barely avoiding the death penalty, Dortell was sentenced to life in prison without the possibility of parole.

Dortell came of age during the Reagan era, when communities were stripped of resources and policing and prisons were boosted. When he began his life sentence, I was a naive college sophomore, a recent immigrant who knew little about the new country I had started to call home and even less about US police and prisons.

Our paths crossed in the early 2000s, when I moved to Southern California and embarked on a journalism career. Dortell heard my daily program on a public radio station in Los Angeles and wrote to me. I wrote back, and we've been friends ever since.

There are millions of Dortells in America, warehoused in myriad state and federal prisons, county jails, immigrant detention centers, and private prisons. They represent the failures of a society built on individualist notions of wealth and privilege, a society that uses deprivation and fear to keep people in line.

Now, at age fifty-seven, Dortell has spent the majority of his life behind bars. Unless California embarks on the project of abolition, he will spend the rest of his life being shuffled around from one institution to another at the whim of the state, forever separated from his daughter and grandchildren and everyone he loves. And to what end?

From the perspective of one who is directly affected by our broken system of policing and prisons, Dortell writes in a letter to me that "the roots of our social problems are never cured because the American philosophy is that crime is an 'individual' phenomenon." He adds, "Society has normalized terms and circumstances such as 'neglected neighborhoods,' 'underprivileged communities,' and the like, making it okay to defund and divest communities that most of us in prison come from."

What would his life have been like had he lived in a world where resources were distributed equitably, where our economies were centered on human well-being rather than inequality? "If I could have avoided adverse circumstances such as redlining, marginalization, and trauma, my life would have been better," he writes. "Poverty and lack of opportunity drive criminality."

Dortell didn't fail anyone. The system that designated him to a life of captivity failed *him*.

In spite of the extreme limitations placed on him during incarceration, Dortell is a published author who has earned six academic degrees and calls himself "a lifelong student." Among his many accomplishments are a paralegal certification obtained in 1995 and a Bachelor of Arts from California State University in Los Angeles earned in 2019. He currently practices trauma-informed care for peers and teaches an array of cognitive behavioral classes in service to those around him. It bears mentioning that his incredible achievements in prison have little to do with how deserving he is of freedom. Maybe he would have been a college professor in a world where he had the resources to thrive. Or maybe he would have been an artist, perfectly content with a life where his needs were being met. In a post-abolitionist world, Dortell's life would have been limited only by his own imagination and drive—as it currently is for privileged elites and as it should be for everyone.

Our political economy fuels inequality, criminalizes poverty, and feeds a voracious incarceration machine that requires exorbitant resources to maintain. It is a structurally unjust system that remains intact only because we as a society cannot imagine another way.

But the thirst for change is strong and it is up to us to channel it into action. The ferocity, size, and scope of the 2020 racial justice uprisings were a robust indicator of public disapproval of this unjust system. For a brief time that year, mass disaffection was accompanied by a concrete demand for solving the crisis of policing and incarceration: Defund the police and fund the things that keep us safe. But news media and politicians successfully diverted the national conversation toward reformism—where good ideas go to die—and momentum is sapped away like air from a deflating balloon.

As a journalist covering social justice movements for twenty-five years, I have seen enthusiasm for change sucked dry over and over again, in part because moneyed elites wear us down with relentless and well-funded messaging and, in part, because we are easily discouraged by the vastness of what is required of us. Left-leaning media outlets, in particular, excel at covering injustice and creating content that leaves the public overwhelmed with information and paralyzed by inaction. My colleagues in the left media tend to feed the notion that too much is wrong with the world and too much is required to right it.

What if, instead, we covered all the ways in which people—like the ones in this book—are addressing the wrongs of policing, courts, and prisons? It isn't enough to scream "Defund the police" or "Abolish prisons." The average American is unlikely to respond positively to such messaging in a vacuum. Even those among us who are disproportionately affected might be reluctant to embrace what feels like a radical upending of how our society is organized.

We know things are broken, but we also know how to fix them and can benefit from the wisdom of the changemakers. We have significantly shifted cultural expectations of race and racial justice. It's now time to back that up with action.

Even before that historic summer when George Floyd's murder lit a fiery spark across the nation, Black-led abolitionist movements had laid the groundwork for change and were implementing nonpolice alternatives to public safety at local levels. Just because the mainstream media—and even many left-leaning media outlets—were not covering these transformative projects, didn't mean they weren't effectively showing what was possible. I began interviewing abolitionists in earnest and wrote reports and essays about imagining police-free worlds, all of which laid the groundwork for this book.

As the abolitionist thinkers in these pages describe, there is a beautiful world awaiting us on the other side of the carceral system. Abolition is an aspiration for a better world, one that is grounded in building community and collective wellness. It articulates a liberatory framework for countless real, living, breathing human beings whose souls remain boxed up and unseen.

Cat Brooks is creating alternative emergency responses to police. Melina Abdullah has influenced her city's budget process, challenging the LA city council to divest from policing and invest in human well-being. Eunisses Hernandez is using her political power to continue the divestment of policing and prisons. Ivette Alé-Ferlito is holding the judiciary accountable. Reina Sultan has outlined clear steps toward abolition for anyone looking for a way forward. Leah Penniman has expanded our imaginations to link abolition with a decarceration of our food and land. Alicia Garza is busy imagining new futures.

It turns out abolition is not a complicated idea. What if all the money that we have poured into policing and prisons had instead been used to mend the social fabric whose holes Dortell slipped through? That's the dream of abolition. Babies born today who would otherwise come of age in a system designed to deprive and incarcerate could instead thrive in a world redesigned to enable thriving communities and foster collective accountability. That transformation is already underway. Abolition is not only desirable, it is achievable.

There is power in seeing what can be realized when one is freed from the stranglehold of colonized imaginations. I truly hope that channeling that power into the pages of this book will help to liberate more imaginations.

ACKNOWLEDGMENTS

I dedicate this book to the millions of human beings this nation has warehoused and forgotten about inside prisons, jails, detention centers, and especially to my friend Dortell Williams who remains trapped in a cage of concrete and the painful limits of society's imagination.

I cannot take credit for conceiving this book. That goes entirely to my editor, Greg Ruggiero, who championed it from start to finish and who offered critical guidance to expanding the conversations around abolition in radically imaginative ways. This is the third book we have worked on together. May our collaboration continue!

I am also grateful to Robin D. G. Kelley for unhesitatingly agreeing to write this book's foreword in spite of the many demands on his time. The critical, historical, and cultural framing he brings beautifully complements the conversations on abolition that appear here. I am deeply humbled by his warm affirmation.

Most of all, I thank the people whose words form the central core of this book—the activists, academics, troublemakers, and visionaries who have inspired me and countless others with their relentless quest to reimagine a social contract centered on humanity and not carceral remedies. In the midst of their busy lives balancing work, activism, childcare, eldercare, school, and organizing, they made space and time for interviews, and, with grace and patience, tolerated my persistent requests for edits, revisions, and final approvals. For years, their ideas inspired and shaped me, challenging me to break free from conventional thinking. In curating their wisdom in this book, I hope they shape and challenge you.

To those members of my family who have to live with me— my husband, children, and parents—thank you for putting up with yet another book project (in spite of my promises that each one will be the last), for listening to me think out loud about the issues this book tackles, and for always cheering me on in spite of it all. I promise the next one will be the last. Maybe.

GET INVOLVED

The following list of abolitionist organizations, networks, and coalitions mentioned throughout this book offer an ideal starting point for getting involved.

8 to Abolition is an offering for abolitionist vision and transformation and a resource for people to build from and incorporate abolitionist demands into local organizing efforts around municipal, state, and federal policies. More information at www.8toabolition.com.

Abolitionist Law Center is a public interest law firm and community organizing project that challenges the criminal punishment system in Pennsylvania. More information at abolitionistlawcenter.org.

Anti Police-Terror Project is a California Bay-Area-based Black-led, multiracial, intergenerational coalition that seeks to build a replicable and sustainable model to eradicate police terror in communities of color. More information at www.antipoliceterrorproject.org.

Black Futures Lab works with Black people to transform communities, build Black political power, and change the way that power operates locally, statewide, and nationally. More information at blackfutureslab.org.

Black Lives Matter Los Angeles became the first chapter of a global network called Black Lives Matter, which was co-founded by Patrisse Cullors, Alicia Garza and Opal Tometi. More information at www.blmla.org.

Black Visions Collective is a Minnesota-based, Black-led, Queer- and Trans-centering organization whose mission is to organize powerful, connected Black communities and dismantle systems of violence. More information at www.blackvisionsmn.org.

Critical Resistance is a national, grassroots organization seeking to build an international movement to end the prison industrial complex by challenging the belief that caging and controlling people makes us safe. More information at critical-resistance.org.

Defund the Police is a one-stop shop for organizers and advocates looking for tools, resources, and trainings to divest from policing and build safer communities. More information at defundpolice.org.

In Our Names Network is a national network of organizations, campaigns, and individuals working to end police violence against Black women, girls, and trans and gender nonconforming people. More information at www.inournamesnetwork.com.

INCITE! is a network of radical feminists of color organizing to end state violence and violence in our homes and communities. More information at incite-national.org.

Interrupting Criminalization offers political education materials, organizing tools, support skill-building, and practice spaces for organizers and movements challenging criminalization and the violence of policing and punishment to build safer communities. More information at www.interruptingcriminalization.com.

JusticeLA Coalition is a Los Angeles-based network that works in partnership with grassroots organizations, advocates, directly impacted communities, and stakeholders to reduce the footprint of incarceration by stopping jail expansion and reclaiming, reimagining, and reinvesting dollars away from incarceration and into community-based systems of care. More information at justicelanow.org.

La Defensa is a femme-led nonprofit advocacy organization dedicated to shifting Los Angeles County's reliance on criminalization and incarceration towards systems of care that center human dignity. More information at ladefensa.org.

Law for Black Lives is a Black-led, queer, abolition-minded, multiracial, feminist and anti-capitalist movement made up of a network of nearly 6,000 radical lawyers and legal advocates whose goal is to support Black organizing and Black movements for liberation through community action. More information at www.law4blacklives.org.

Movement for Black Lives was created as a space for Black organizations across the country to debate and discuss the current political conditions, develop shared assessments of what political interventions are necessary in order to achieve key policy, cultural, and political wins, and convene organizational leadership in order to debate and cocreate a shared movement-wide strategy. More information at m4bl.org.

People's Budget LA is a coalition convened by Black Lives Matter Los Angeles that is focused on including the people in the city budgeting process. More information at peoplesbudgetla.com.

Policing Alternatives and Diversion Initiative is an Atlanta-based organization, born out of the work and vision of Atlantans directly impacted by policing and incarceration and committed to a new approach to community safety and wellness. More information at www.atlantapad.org.

Prison Radio is an independent multimedia production studio centered on the voices of people most impacted by the prison industrial complex. More information at www.prisonradio.org.

Reimagine LA County is a coalition of advocates, community organizations, and neighbors calling for a ballot measure to divest from incarceration and policing and invest in the health and economic wellness of marginalized people in their communities. More information at reimagine.la.

Soul Fire Farm is an Afro-Indigenous centered community farm committed to uprooting racism and seeding sovereignty in the food system. More information at www.soulfirefarm.org.

NOTES

1. Shaka N'Zinga, *A Disjointed Search for the Will to Live* (New York: Soft Skull Press, 2003).
2. Benjamin Drew, *A North-Side View of Slavery. The Refugee: or the Narratives of Fugitive Slaves in Canada. Related by Themselves, with an Account of the History and Condition of the Colored Population of Upper Canada* (Boston: John P. Jewett and Company, 1856), 30.
3. Perspectives on Community Safety from Black America, Movement for Black Lives, GenForward, December 5, 2023.
4. M.C. Brown II and Camille Lloyd, "Black Americans Less Confident, Satisfied With Local Police," Gallup, September 18, 2023.
5. Michelle Alexander, *The New Jim Crow: Mass Incarceration in the Age of Colorblindness* (New York: The New Press, 2010), 2.
6. Khalil Gibran Muhammad, *The Condemnation of Blackness: Race, Crime, and the Making of Modern Urban America* (Cambridge: Harvard University Press, 2019), xii.
7. Larry Buchanan, Quoctrung Bui and Jugal K. Patel, "Black Lives Matter May Be the Largest Movement in U.S. History," *New York Times*, July 3, 2020; The Major Cities Chiefs Association, "REPORT ON THE 2020 PROTESTS AND CIVIL UNREST," October 2020, 1.
8. See MappingPoliceViolence.org, "Police Killed 1,347 People in the United States in 2023," Accessed February, 2023.
9. 55 Facts About Mass Incarceration, Prison Policy Initiative, updated April 2023.
10. Interview with Black Visions, *Stanford Journal of Civil Rights & Civil Liberties*, March 4, 2022, Volume 17, Special Issue, 549.
11. Angela Y. Davis, *Are Prisons Obsolete?* (New York: Seven Stories Press, Open Media Series, 2003), 4.
12. Rachel Kushner, "Is Prison Necessary? Ruth Wilson Gilmore Might Change Your Mind," *New York Times Magazine*, April 17, 2019.
13. Keeanga-Yamahtta Taylor, "The Emerging Movement for Police and Prison Abolition," *The New Yorker*, May 7, 2021.

14. Hanna Phifer, "For Angela Davis and Gina Dent, Abolition Is the Only Way," *Harper's Bazaar*, January 4, 2022.

15. Sonali Kolhatkar, "Supreme Court Orders California Prison System to Relieve Overcrowding," *Uprising*, June 1, 2011.

16. Heather Long and Andrew Van Dam, "The black-white economic divide is as wide as it was in 1968," *Washington Post*, June 4, 2020.

17. See Vera.com, "What Policing Costs: A Look at Spending in America's Biggest Cities," Accessed December 12, 2023.

18. Sahil Kapur, "Democratic leaders clash with Black Lives Matter activists over 'defund the police,'" NBCNews.com, June 8, 2020.

19. "Perspectives on Community Safety from Black America, Movement for Black Lives," GenForward, December 5, 2023.

20. Los Angeles Times Editorial Board, "L.A.'s key justice reform survives court challenge. Time to pick up the pace," *Los Angeles Times*, August 7, 2023.

21. Asha DuMonthier, Chandra Childers, and Jessica Milli, "The Status of Black Women in the United States," Institute for Women's Policy Research, 2020.

22. Angela Y. Davis, *Are Prisons Obsolete?* (New York: Seven Stories Press, Open Media Series, 2003), 9.

23. Tammy Mutasa, "Seattle Police budget shrinks after City Council's final approval," KOMO News, November 22, 2021.

24. Cate Corcoran, "Giving Prisoners Some Air," Stanford Magazine, July/August 2001.

25. Joy James, *In Pursuit of Revolutionary Love Precarity, Power, Communities*, (United Kingdom: Divided, 2022), 6.

26. Reina Sultan, "How Transformative Justice Responds to Violence Without the Carceral System," Shadowproof, July 27, 2020.

27. Davey D, "Oscar Grant, young father and peacemaker, executed by BART police," *San Francisco Bay View*, January 6, 2009.

28. John Ramos, "Oakland crisis center opens to handle mental emergencies without police help," CBS Bay Area, January 14, 2023.

29. Kimberly Veklerov, "Oakland Mayor Libby Schaaf wins race for re-election," *San Francisco Chronicle*, November 7, 2018.

30. Rick Rojas, Neelam Bohra, Eliza Fawcett and Emily Cochrane, "What We Know About Tyre Nichols's Lethal Encounter With Memphis Police," *New York Times*, November 2, 2023.

31. Sam Levin, "'Unsung hero': the baker and activist whose death inspired calls for restorative justice," *The Guardian*, February 18, 2023.

32. Max Matza, "Tyre Nichols: What is the 'Scorpion' unit of Memphis police?" BBC.com, January 29, 2023.

33. ArLuther Lee, "Police shoot, kill 18-year-old Hispanic security guard on patrol at LA auto shop," *Atlanta Journal Constitution*, June 24, 2020.

34. Jeong Park, Laura Newberry, Julia Wick, "Police forcibly remove BLM-L.A. leader, a Cal State L.A. professor, from campus mayoral debate," *Los Angeles Times*, May 1, 2022.

35. Meryl Kornfield, "Cornel West announces BLM activist, professor Melina Abdullah as VP pick," *Washington Post*, April 10, 2024.

36. Tyler Kingkade, "Los Angeles activists were already pushing to defund the police. Then George Floyd died." NBC News, June 15, 2020.

37. David Zahniser, Julia Wick, Benjamin Oreskes, Dakota Smith, and Gustavo Arellano, "Racist remarks in leaked audio of L.A. council members spark outrage, disgust," *Los Angeles Times*, October 9, 2022.

38. Aaron Morrison, "Black Lives Matter movement marks 10 years of activism and renews its call to defund the police, AP, July 12, 2023.

39. Patrisse Cullors, Black Lives Matter began after Trayvon Martin's death. Ferguson showed its staying power," NBC News, January 1, 2020.

40. Larry Buchanan, Quoctrung Bui and Jugal K. Patel, "Black Lives Matter May Be the Largest Movement in U.S. History, *New York Times*, July 3, 2020.

41. Cation exchange capacity (CEC) is a measure of the total negative charges within the soil that bind to plant nutrient cations such as calcium (Ca2+), magnesium (Mg2+) and potassium (K+). As such, the CEC is a property of a soil that describes its capacity to supply nutrient cations to the soil solution for plant uptake.